I0605569

JUST A MINUTE

Why Humans Tell Time

Kirstie Hudson *and*
Monique Polak

Illustrated by
Paige Stampatori

ORCA BOOK PUBLISHERS

Published in Canada and the United States in 2025 by Orca Book Publishers.
orcabook.com

Library and Archives Canada Cataloguing in Publication
Title: Just a minute : why humans tell time / Kirstie Hudson and Monique Polak ; illustrated by Paige Stampatori.
Names: Hudson, Kirstie, author | Polak, Monique, author | Stampatori, Paige, illustrator.
Series: Orca timeline ; 12.
Description: Series statement: Orca timeline ; 12 | Includes bibliographical references and index.
Identifiers: Canadiana (print) 20240490568 | Canadiana (ebook) 20240490576 |
ISBN 9781459840621 (hardcover) | ISBN 9781459840638 (PDF) | ISBN 9781459840645 (EPUB)
Subjects: LCSH: Time—Juvenile literature. | LCSH: Time measurements—Juvenile literature. | LCGFT: Informational works.
Classification: LCC QB209.5 .H83 2025 | DDC j529/.7—dc23

Library of Congress Control Number: 2024947809

Summary: Part of the nonfiction Orca Timeline series for middle-grade readers, this illustrated book is a comprehensive overview of time, and how and why we measure it.

Orca Book Publishers is committed to reducing the consumption of nonrenewable resources in the production of our books. We make every effort to use materials that support a sustainable future.

Orca Book Publishers gratefully acknowledges the support for its publishing programs provided by the following agencies: the Government of Canada, the Canada Council for the Arts and the Province of British Columbia through the BC Arts Council and the Book Publishing Tax Credit.

Cover and interior artwork by Paige Stampatori.
Design by Dahlia Yuen.
Edited by Vivian Sinclair.

Printed and bound in South Korea.

28 27 26 25 • 1 2 3 4

To my family; there's nothing better than spending time with you. —K.H.

To Nadine Lucille Rouleau. Because I love your cheeks and because when I'm with you, time flies! —M.P.

The Prague Orloj is an astronomical clock installed in the city's Old Town Hall in 1410. It's made up of an astronomical dial, which shows the position of the sun and moon, a calendar dial and a clock dial.
NIKADA/GETTY IMAGES

CONTENTS

INTRODUCTION 1

ONE 5
It All Started with Chronos

TWO 15
Hours, Minutes, Seconds

THREE 25
Water Clocks and Pocket Watches

FOUR 37
It's What's Inside That Counts

FIVE 47
Can Your Dog—or Your Houseplant—Tell Time?

SIX 57
Hurry Up and Slow Down!

SEVEN 69
Running Out of Time

GLOSSARY 81

RESOURCES 83

ACKNOWLEDGMENTS 84

INDEX 85

zZZ

INTRODUCTION

Time is one of the most-used words in the English language. Think about all the different ways you use it every day. There's lunchtime, dinnertime, bedtime, good times, serving time, killing time, keeping time, buying time, time-out, time travel, overtime, free time...and the list goes on. We humans spend a lot of time thinking about time. And because of technology we can know the exact time every second of the day.

But time is about more than numbers. Our perception of time can be different from actual clock time. Time can move too quickly, or it can pass very, very slowly. On the one hand, when you're having fun, time flies. On the other hand, it almost stands still when you're waiting for a test to end or for your next birthday to arrive. Sometimes you feel like the tortoise, and sometimes you feel like the hare. Often we want more time—there never seems to be enough of it to get everything done. There's school, and soccer practice, and homework, and walking the dog—and what about time with friends?

Marking Time

Our ancient ancestors first measured time by looking to the sun and moon. The invention of clocks and other time-telling devices led to our being able to measure even the smallest amount of time, the ***zeptosecond***. We can also look inside ourselves—our brains have their own internal clocks. In nature, animals have their own sense of time and rely on natural cycles to help them survive. But measuring time was just a start. Humans soon recognized the need to manipulate time.

Daylight saving time was introduced to give us more daylight hours to get things done. Recently the United States Senate passed a bill, called the Sunshine Protection Act, to abolish the practice of moving the clock back in the fall and forward in the spring. If this becomes law, it is expected that other countries, including Canada, will follow suit.

Yet, try as we will, humans will never be able to control time. None of us will be here forever. That thought might strike you as depressing. But the fact that we don't have forever makes every moment of our time on Earth more precious. Our planet needs us too. There's no time to waste if we want to address problems such as global warming and ensure the future of our planet. There's so much to learn about this timely subject. So let's get going. The clock is ticking!

Zeptoseconds

The zeptosecond is the shortest unit of time that has ever been measured. In 2016 scientists at Goethe University in Germany measured the amount of time it takes for a particle of light (a photon) to cross the tiny space occupied by a hydrogen molecule. The answer they came up with was about 247 zeptoseconds. How fast is a zeptosecond? It's a trillionth of a billionth of a second!

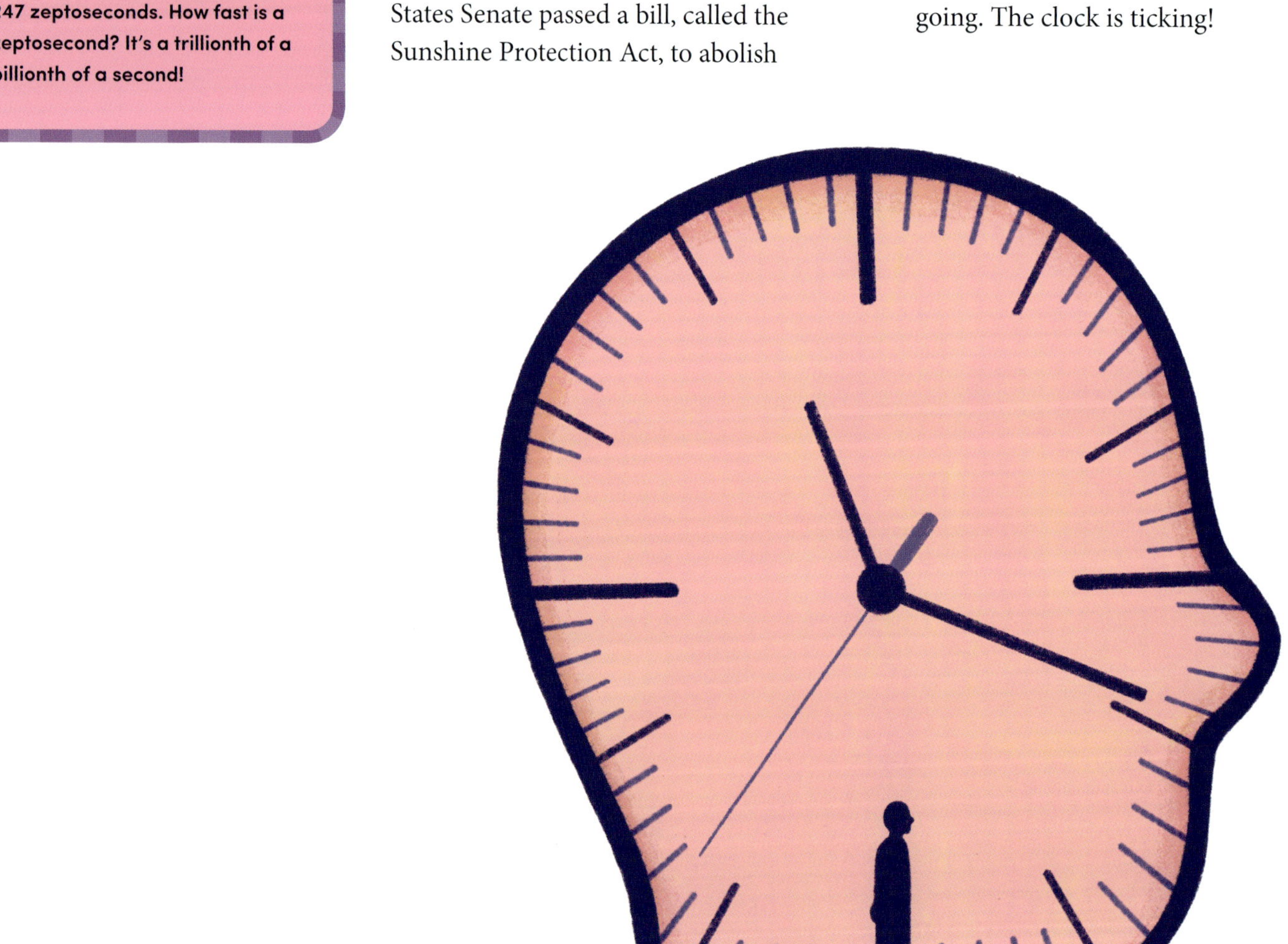

Ready, set, *go*!
SOLSTOCK/GETTY IMAGES

1865
Alice's Adventures in Wonderland
A Wrinkle in Time
1962
A Wrinkle in Time
1985
Back to the Future
1625
Father Time
700 BCE
Chronos, Aiôn and Kaïros

ONE

IT ALL STARTED WITH CHRONOS

"Have I got a story for you!" The urge to share stories is as old as humankind. As far back as the Paleolithic period—which started about 2.5 million years ago—early humans used cave drawings to tell stories. We tell them to connect with others. But storytelling is also a way for us to grapple with life's big questions, such as, What is time? How can we make the most of the time we have?

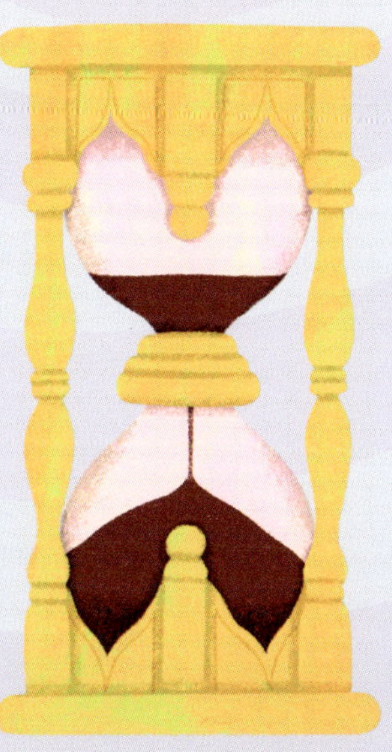

The Gods of Time

Chronos, Aiôn and Kaïros | Ancient Greece |  700 BCE

It's a Myth

Mythology is a body of traditional stories from a group of people. The stories illustrate how they see the world and natural phenomena and explain their beliefs and practices. Some myths have been around for thousands of years. They have survived for so long because they let us visit other worlds and meet fascinating characters. They also help us make sense of our world and ourselves.

Have you ever heard of Hercules, who was known for his heroic strength? Hercules was probably not a real guy. He is a figure from Greek ***mythology***. The ancient Greeks understood that time is a complicated subject. That may explain why they came up with three gods connected to time. Meet Chronos, Aiôn and Kaïros.

In ancient Greek art, Chronos is depicted as an elderly bearded man. He often carries a scythe (a farming implement) and sometimes an ***hourglass***. For the ancient Greeks, Chronos represented linear time—the past, present and future. In other words, time that ticks.

Aiôn represented time's cycles. He was connected to the seasons and later to the afterlife. Like all people who farm, the ancient Greeks needed to know when to plant and when to harvest their crops. Because he is associated with cycles, Aiôn is sometimes depicted as young, other times as elderly.

You may have heard the expression *When the time is right*. For the ancient Greeks, Kaïros is connected with ***opportunistic time***. Compost-bin pickup day is an opportunistic time for hungry raccoons, since that's when we put out our food scraps. Kaïros is also associated with something called ***deep time***. Unlike the ticking sort of time, deep time happens when we lose track of time altogether. This sense of deep time—that time seems to have stopped—tends to happen when we feel connected with our surroundings or with people we care about. You might experience deep time when you are snowshoeing in the woods, reading an amazing book or doing an art project with your best friend.

MALCOLM P CHAPMAN/GETTY IMAGES

More Hands Than a Clock

Most clocks have two hands—a short one to indicate the hour and a longer one to indicate the minute. (Some have a third for seconds.) Kali, the Hindu goddess of time and death, is usually depicted as having four arms and hands. In paintings Kali often has blue or black skin and fangs—and she's usually sticking out her tongue! Kali represents female strength and motherhood. Like all moms, Kali has the power to give life. But watch out! This goddess can also destroy life. That's how Kali embodies time.

Zoroastrians' Take on Time

Zoroastrianism is one of the world's oldest religions still in existence. It originated in Persia (now called Iran) and has been around for nearly 4,000 years. According to Zoroastrianism, there are two kinds of time: infinite and finite. Infinite time is eternal and unchanging, without a beginning or an end. Finite time is divided into the past and the future, and it is subject to change. Zoroastrians believe that time (and space) are God's trap to hold on to and destroy evil forces. They divide each day into five parts, or gehs, for prayer and ritual. Zoroastrians refrain from prayer between midnight and 1:00 a.m. because they believe evil forces are most powerful in that hour.

REBECCAPICARD/GETTY IMAGES

A Zoroastrian fire temple in Yazd, Iran. The religion gets its name from its founder, the prophet Zoroaster.
NANTONOV/GETTY IMAGES

Norns of the Norse

Urd  Scandinavia 800

If you read Marvel comics, you may have heard of Urd, a character in the Thor series. Or you may know her from the Japanese animanga TV series *Oh My Goddess!* But Urd was not invented by Marvel or the Japanese animanga industry. She comes to us via Norse mythology.

The Vikings, also known as Norsemen, were Scandinavian seafaring explorers, warriors, traders and settlers. They traveled the seas from about the late 8th to the early 11th centuries, conquering much of Europe. For the ancient Norse, Urd was the goddess of time. Also known as Urth, she was one of three Norns, or fates. Urd represented the past. Her sister Skuld represented the future, while her other sister, Verdandi, the present. The sisters lived in the well of fate at the base of Yggdrasil, the sacred tree of life. The Norse people believed their fates were determined at birth.

The three Norns used jugs to draw water from the well of fate to nourish the sacred tree of life.
BAUHAUS1000/GETTY IMAGES

Father Time Gets Around

The Triumph of Truth by Peter Paul Rubens

Antwerp, Belgium  1625

You don't have to be into mythology to have heard of Father Time. He's part of ***popular culture***. Sometimes he hangs out with Mother Nature. Father Time is usually depicted as having a gray beard and carrying an hourglass or scythe. Sound familiar? Father Time is believed to have been modeled on Chronos.

Father Time has been personifying time for about 500 years. Back in 1625 Flemish painter Peter Paul Rubens completed a giant oil painting about the struggle between truth and lies. He called it *The Triumph of Truth*. In the painting, which now hangs at the Louvre Museum in Paris, Truth is a beautiful young woman who is rescued by Time. We'd recognize his gray beard anywhere! Rubens wanted to tell us that with time, truth wins out over lies.

It's Popular

The term *popular culture* refers to cultural information we may not learn at school or during a museum visit. That's because we absorb popular culture from popular sources—like comics, movies and TV.

MAEMANEE/SHUTTERSTOCK.COM

Father Time and the Mad Tea Party

Alice's Adventures in Wonderland by Lewis Carroll | Oxford, England |  1865

Father Time was not invited to the mad tea party in Lewis Carroll's children's book *Alice's Adventures in Wonderland*. But Father Time comes up in the conversation between Alice, the Mad Hatter, the March Hare and the Dormouse. When Alice complains that the others are wasting time, the Mad Hatter gets annoyed. "If you knew Time as well as I do," he tells Alice, "you wouldn't talk about wasting *it*. It's *him*."

One of the many things that makes the tea party mad is that time has stopped. It's always six o'clock! Or as the Mad Hatter says, "It's always tea-time, and we've no time to wash the things."

Carroll does more than make us laugh. He explores the question of time. Haven't we all wished—perhaps on a sleepy Sunday afternoon, or while roasting marshmallows at our favorite campsite (without mosquitoes!)—that we could stop time? That we could make a happy moment last forever? But, Carroll reminds us, there would be a downside. You'd get bored of napping on a never-ending Sunday. Marshmallows would stop tasting good if you ate too many, and you'd end up having to drink from a dirty cup at the never-ending tea party!

The Hatter (usually referred to as the Mad Hatter) is a Lewis Carroll character known for his top hat and wacky sense of humor.

CAREY RUSSELL PHOTOGRAPHY/GETTY IMAGES

A Time-Travel Tale

A Wrinkle in Time by Madeleine L'Engle | New York, United States |  1962

There's another wish many of us have related to time. If only we could travel back and forth through time. Wouldn't it be interesting to pay a visit to the early humans who made cave drawings? Or have a peek at life on Earth in the year 4000? Some stories let us travel—at least in our imaginations—back to the past or into the future.

One children's book about time travel is Madeleine L'Engle's *A Wrinkle in Time*. Published in 1962 the book was made into a movie for the big screen in 2018.

In this science fiction fantasy for kids, three youngsters—Meg Murry, her kid brother Charles Wallace and a friend, Calvin O'Keefe, embark on an exciting and sometimes frightening journey through time and space. The siblings' dad, a physicist, has mysteriously disappeared. He was an expert on tesseracts—four-dimensional cubes—which he believed could make time travel possible. The children's goal is to rescue him and defeat an evil force that has found its way into several worlds.

"The best evidence we have that time travel is not possible, and never will be, is that we have not been invaded by hordes of tourists from the future."

—**Stephen Hawking,** scientist and author

This sculpture of a tesseract was created by Spanish architect Miguel Ángel Ruiz-Larrea.
OSCAR GONZALEZ FUENTES/SHUTTERSTOCK.COM

Movies Get In On the Time-Travel Craze

Back to the Future Movie · Hill Valley, California · 1985

One movie classic about time travel is *Back to the Future*. This science fiction film came out in 1985 and stars Canadian-born actor and activist Michael J. Fox. In the movie, set in the fictional town of Hill Valley, California, Fox plays a teenager named Marty McFly. Marty befriends Doc Brown, a mad scientist who claims to have transformed a DeLorean automobile into a time machine. Marty uses it to travel back in time to 1955, when his parents were teenagers.

Back in Time

Screenwriter Bob Gale got the idea for *Back to the Future* when he found his father's high school yearbook and wondered if he and his father would have been friends had they been teenagers at the same time. Gale realized the only way he would be able to answer this question was by traveling back in time—which is exactly what Gale and his screenwriting partner Robert Zemeckis allowed Marty McFly to do in their movie. Proof that in the world of imagination, anything is possible!

HETHERS/SHUTTERSTOCK.COM

ART KONOVALOV/SHUTTERSTOCK.COM

This surreal illustration of a spiral clock in space makes you wonder about time, space, life and death.
AMGUN/SHUTTERSTOCK.COM

Curiouser and Curiouser

The Curious Case of Benjamin Button Movie
New Orleans, Louisiana 2008

The Curious Case of Benjamin Button also tackles the subject of time travel. Based on a short story written by F. Scott Fitzgerald and published in 1922, the movie stars Brad Pitt and Cate Blanchett. It begins with an incredible twist—Benjamin Button is born a wrinkled old man. His mother dies shortly afterward, and his father abandons him. Instead of aging the way the rest of us do, Benjamin ages *backward*. So while everyone around him grows older, he gets younger.

Benjamin Button teaches us that age is far more than a number—it's how we feel inside. As he reminds us, "For what it's worth, it's never too late or, in my case, too early to be whoever you want to be."

All these myths, books and movies that grapple with the subject of time are proof of its importance to us and our eternal curiosity about its meaning. One thing we know for certain is there's no stopping the progression of time—and our time on this planet will come to an end. It's an important reminder to consider how we want to spend the time that we do have.

C.15,000 BCE
Lunar calendars
1880
Greenwich
Mean Time
FUTURE
Coordinated
Lunar Time
2000 BCE
Sunlight and Shadows
1949
First atomic
clock

TWO

HOURS, MINUTES, SECONDS

Chances are, your first thought when you woke up today had something to do with time. Do I have time to sleep in a little later? Will I be on time for school? How much time is left before I have to hand in my social studies project?

It's easy to find out what time it is every hour, minute and second of the day. We carry time in our pockets. But our earliest ancestors marked time differently. They observed the world around them and saw how natural cycles—like changing seasons, annual floods and animal births—repeated on a predictable cycle. This told them the best times to travel or hunt and forage. The ability to measure time became more sophisticated when they observed the phases of the moon and the constellations in the sky to mark yearly, monthly or weekly events. Time was broken down even further when humans started measuring time using the sun, dividing a day into hours, then hours into seconds, milliseconds and zeptoseconds.

"How did it get so late so soon?"

—Dr. Seuss, author and cartoonist

Let Me Check My Lunar Calendar

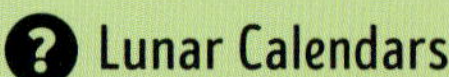
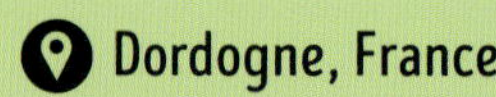

Lunar Calendars | Dordogne, France | c. 15,000 BCE

In 1940 four teenagers discovered the Lascaux cave in France. Inside, archaeologists discovered early human skeletons, tools and prehistoric cave art, including a painting thought to be one of the oldest lunar calendars ever found. Michael Rappenglueck, a researcher from the University of Munich, claims the 15,000-year-old group of dots and squares painted among other animals, including horses and bulls, shows the phases of the moon.

Discoveries of mammoth tusks engraved with patterns of short and long notches are also thought to be examples of early lunar calendars. Archaeologists believe the lines show the phases of the moon over one year and are evidence of how early humans marked the passage of time. They are designed to be carried on journeys like hunting trips or seasonal ***migrations***.

At another archaeological site near Mezin, in Ukraine, early humans are thought to have made a lunar calendar that could be worn on their bodies, like the first smartwatch. A bracelet made of mammoth ivory was discovered at the site. It's wide and thick and covered in geometric designs. The patterns show the phases of the moon and sun over 280 days. Thousands of years after those first lunar calendars, this method of marking time was still in use—to predict the best times for planting and harvesting crops and for organizing public events like the mid-autumn Moon Festival. This festival has been celebrated in China for more than 3,000 years, and it always happens on the day when the moon is at its brightest and fullest size.

Waxing, Waning, Rising and Setting

Each month of a lunar calendar is based on a full cycle of the moon's phases, usually starting with the new moon, then the quarter moon, the full moon and, finally, the third-quarter moon. In between these main phases are times when the moon is waxing (getting bigger) or waning (getting smaller). It takes about 29.5 days for the moon to complete its cycle. An example of a lunar calendar still in use today is the Islamic, or Hijri, calendar, introduced in 622. It includes four holy months and Ramadan, the month of fasting.

The calendar used in most parts of the world today is the Gregorian. It's a solar calendar based on the time it takes Earth to rotate once around the sun, or 365 and ¼ days. It was introduced in 1582.

DELPIXEL/SHUTTERSTOCK.COM

If you leave your phone at home, you can still check the time by the sun's position in the sky. When the sun is directly overhead, that means it's noon and time for lunch.
OS TARTAROUCHOS/GETTY IMAGES

It All Adds Up

 Sexagesimal Number System  Ancient Sumer 3000 BCE

It takes one year for Earth to orbit the sun. It takes a month for the moon to orbit Earth. A week represents one of the moon's four phases—each phase is a seven-day period so together the four phases correspond to the roughly 29-day lunar month. A day is how long it takes Earth to rotate once on its axis. For thousands of years ancient civilizations used these guides to measure the major units of time in their world. But where did hours, minutes and seconds come from?

We have the ancient Sumerians to thank for the number 60 that minutes and seconds are based on. Their sexagesimal, or base 60, number system came from how they counted using their hands. Sumerians used the thumb on their right hand to count the three parts of each of the other four fingers on the same hand. When they got to 12, they raised one finger on the left hand to mark their place. Five fingers times 12 equals 60.

24 Hours

The ancient Egyptians gave us the number 12 (for hours in the day) as they divided the period between sunrise and sunset into 12 equal parts (12 for day and 12 for night, making 24), but the parts depended on the amount of sunlight and the time of year. So if it was summer, the "hours" were longer, and if it was winter, they were shorter. And what happened on the days when you couldn't see the sun? Well, they would simply guess at the time. The idea of time was more fluid in the ancient world—hours could stretch or shrink in ways they don't today. It gives a new meaning to the phrase *Can I stay up just a little bit longer?*

ZHENGJIE WU/GETTY IMAGES

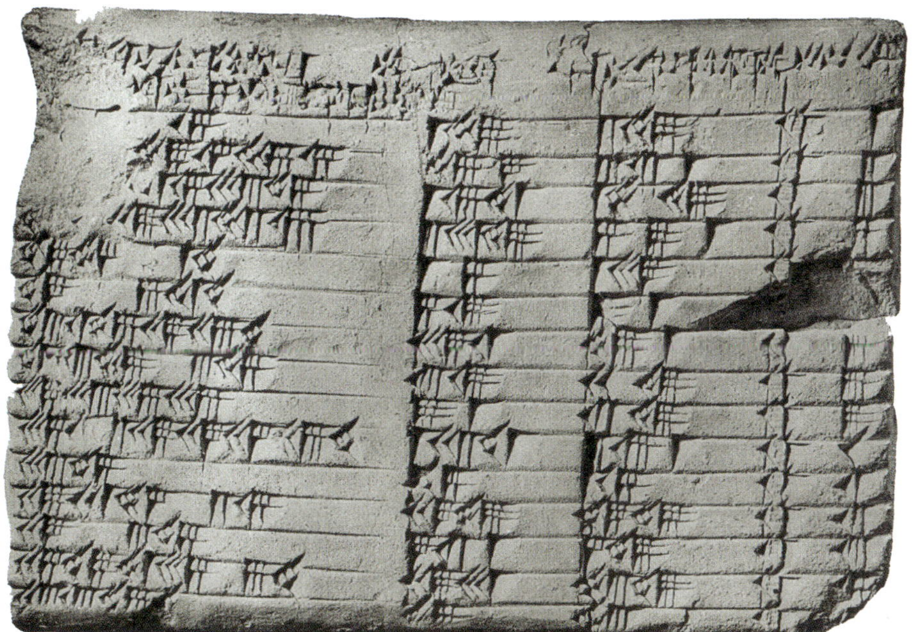

1
2
3
4
5
6
7
8
9
10

The Babylonian clay tablet Plimpton 322 is inscribed with cuneiform numbers written in the sexagesimal system. Experts believe the tablet, which dates to 1800 BCE, was used to calculate how to construct temples and canals.
(LEFT) WIKIMEDIA COMMONS/PUBLIC DOMAIN; (RIGHT) JOSELL7/WIKIMEDIA COMMONS/CC BY-SA 4.0

The length of a shadow is determined by the sun's position in the sky. Shadows are the longest in the early morning and early evening, when the sun is low on the horizon.
JORN GEORG TOMTER/GETTY IMAGES

Here Comes the Sun

Sunlight and Shadows
Ancient Babylon | **2000 BCE**

While the phases of the moon could help people mark major yearly, monthly and weekly events, they used the position of the sun to divide time over the course of a single day. In ancient Babylon buildings were constructed facing the sun so that their shadow could mark the time as it traveled along the ground. Almost any object could be used to follow the sun's position and show the passage of time, from a person to a stick, tree or even the Pyramids of Giza.

You need direct sunlight to tell the time using the sun. Once the clouds roll in, it's time to check your phone.
CATHERINE FALLS COMMERCIAL/GETTY IMAGES

Let's Meet at Six Feet

***The Ecclesiazusae* by Aristophanes**
Ancient Greece |  **391 BCE**

In ancient Greece people needed to know when to meet at the agora (a public meeting place) to discuss the important business of the day. They didn't have watches to set the hour, so they used the length of the shadow cast by a person's body, measuring it in feet or even shoes. Instead of scheduling meetings for, say, 8:30 a.m., as we do today, they might be set for 6, 8, 10 or 12 feet. Once the sun set, no decisions could be made, as the time couldn't be measured. And it wasn't just meetings that had to be scheduled—there were also more practical considerations. Aristophanes was a Greek playwright. In his play *The Ecclesiazusae*, a woman complains that all her husband does all day is watch his own shadow until it reaches 10 feet. That's when he knows it's time to eat dinner!

It wasn't until the invention of the first clocks in the 13th century that humans started measuring time without having to rely on the sun. That meant it could also be measured precisely in smaller units like minutes and seconds.

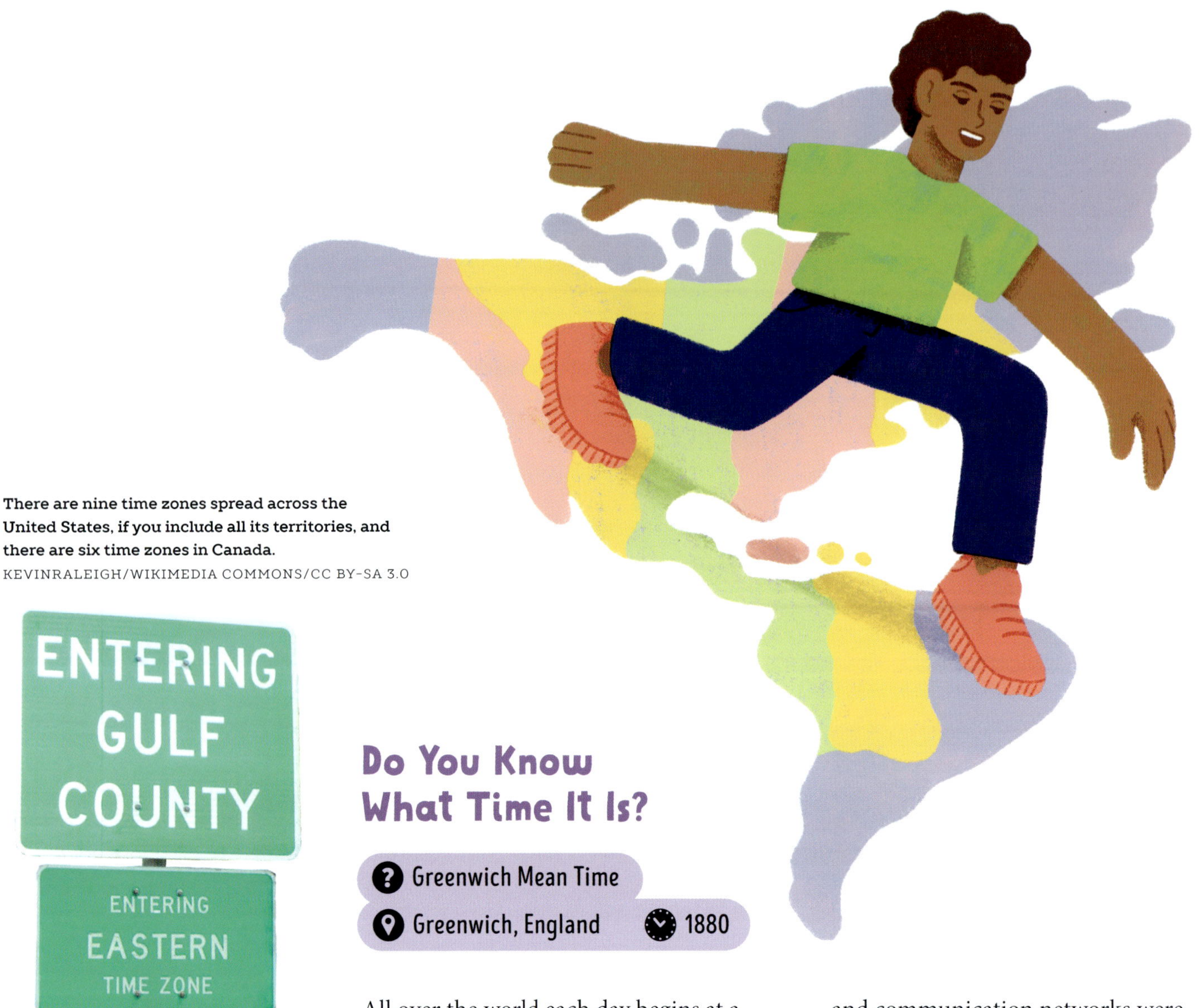

There are nine time zones spread across the United States, if you include all its territories, and there are six time zones in Canada.
KEVINRALEIGH/WIKIMEDIA COMMONS/CC BY-SA 3.0

Do You Know What Time It Is?

? Greenwich Mean Time
Greenwich, England 1880

All over the world each day begins at a different time. If you live in Toronto you can't call your aunt in New Delhi when you get home from school because it's 2:30 a.m. where she lives, and she wouldn't be happy if you woke her up. New Delhi is always 10.5 hours ahead of Toronto. Similarly if it's 8:00 p.m. in New York City, then we know it's 5:00 p.m. in Vancouver and 9:00 a.m. tomorrow morning in Shanghai. That's because today there are 24 time zones in the world to match the 24 hours in a day.

This idea of standard times around the world is relatively new—it was only developed in the mid-19th century. In Great Britain, railway and communication networks were growing, and the companies needed a way to make railroad timetables less confusing. Customers needed to know their train was going to show up at 10:00 a.m. if that's what it said on the schedule. The railway companies adopted ***Greenwich Mean Time (GMT)***—the local mean time at the Royal Observatory in Greenwich, England—as the single standard time across their network. It worked so well that a few years later, all the clocks in the country were also set to that time, and in 1880 GMT became the legal standard time in Great Britain. It's still used today as a time zone in some European and African countries.

Set Your Watches

In 1972 Coordinated Universal Time (UTC) replaced GMT. It's not a time zone but rather a worldwide time standard used to regulate clocks and time zones based on Earth's rotation and on readings from around 400 ***atomic clocks***, which measure the precise length of one second.

When you're traveling between time zones, a smartwatch can automatically update to the time in your location. If you have a traditional watch, you'll have to remember to set the time forward or backward.
NATALIA LEBEDINSKAIA/GETTY IMAGES

Wait a Second

International Bureau of Weights and Measures | Paris, France |  2030

Scientists are looking for an even more precise way to measure a second, which has been calculated the same way since 1967. That's when the international standard for defining a second became based on the vibrations of a cesium atom in an atomic clock. The problem with atomic clocks is that they eventually lose time. For example, the NIST-F1 atomic clock in Boulder, Colorado, would gain or lose a second over 20 million years. It doesn't sound like a big problem, but things like ***GPS***, telecommunications and systems to predict earthquakes and volcanoes need the most exact time possible. Using new laser technology, scientists today can get even more precise measurements (or ticks) inside atoms and therefore a better measure of time (an error of one second in every 300 million years). The International Bureau of Weights and Measures is an organization made up of 64 member countries that work together on matters related to the science and standards of measurement, including the second. Their study of these new optical atomic clocks means we could have a new way to measure a second by 2030.

What Is Time, Really?

Time is a measurable period in which an action, process or condition exists or continues from the past through the present and into the future.
—Merriam-Webster Dictionary

An early version of the atomic clock. It was a game changer in measuring precise units of time.

NATIONAL PHYSICAL LABORATORY/WIKIMEDIA COMMONS/PUBLIC DOMAIN

What Time Is It on the Moon?

Coordinated Lunar Time | The Moon | Future

We're really good at managing time here on Earth, but when we leave the planet, things get a little more complicated. The White House asked the National Aeronautics and Space Administration (NASA) to develop a plan for a time zone on the moon—Coordinated Lunar Time. Right now, any mission to the moon is set to the time zone of where it's from—Moscow, Beijing or Houston, for example. But with many more missions to the moon planned for the future, different countries will have to work together, and they can't do that if they're all on different time zones. Scientists are still figuring out the details of how it will work. The challenge is that clocks move faster on the moon than here on Earth because of the difference in gravity (clocks move more slowly in stronger gravitational fields).

NASA's Space Communications and Navigation (SCaN) program is developing a Coordinated Lunar Time system that could be used not just on the moon, but on Mars and other planets or stars in our solar system.

MASTER/GETTY IMAGES

1600 BCE
Water clock

8TH CENTURY
Hour Glass

1969
First quartz watch

10
1883
Digital clock

6:30

EXPO'70
TIME CAPSULE
2100
Plutonium clock

THREE

WATER CLOCKS AND POCKET WATCHES

"What time is it?" It's a question we ask a lot, and there are many timekeeping devices to provide the answer. We can check the time on a cell phone or computer, a ***digital clock*** (there may be one on your stove or microwave), a wall clock, a quartz watch (if you know someone who still wears one) or a smartwatch. Humans have always wanted to know the time. How else could we make plans or know if we were running late? But considering how long we've been around, cell phones, computers, digital-display clocks and even wall clocks and watches are relatively recent inventions.

Hello, Sunshine!

Shadow Clock  Egypt  c. 3500 BCE

As you read in chapter 2, the first timekeeping device was a simple stick planted in the ground. This ***shadow clock***, or sun stick, was invented by ancient Egyptians and Babylonians, who noted the changes in the shadow cast by the stick. The position of the shadow helped people determine the approximate time. Approximate because, like most early time-telling devices, the shadow clock was far from precise.

Like the shadow clock, a ***sundial*** measures time by the length or direction of a shadow caused by the sun. Sundials were flat and made of wood or some kind of stone, like limestone. A long stick called a gnomon was inserted in a hole, and the length of the shadow it cast indicated time of day. What differentiates a sundial from a shadow clock is that a sundial has lines or markings on its dial to indicate the time.

It's believed that the oldest sundial comes from a tomb in the Valley of the Kings, the burial ground for the ancient Egyptian pharaohs. The sundial was found in one of the stone huts used by construction workers at the site and dates to 1500 BCE. There are 12 even spaces marked on the limestone, but archaeologists can only guess at what the workers were marking. Were they counting down the hours until the end of their workday? For thousands of years the sundial was the world's most popular timekeeping device. Its main disadvantage was that it only worked on sunny days!

Ancient sundials are divided into 12 sections set 15 degrees apart. That's because it takes about one hour for the sun to move that distance in the sky.
RUDOLPHOUS/WIKIMEDIA COMMONS/CC BY-SA 4.0

Taipei 101

This skyscraper was completed in 2004. The park beside the tower is designed to be the base of a massive sundial that uses the shadow from the skyscraper to tell time. At the time of this writing, it was the world's tallest unofficial sundial.

ALTON/WIKIMEDIA COMMONS/ CC BY-SA 3.0

Drip, Drip, Drip

Water Clock | Babylon, Mesopotamia | 1600 BCE

The clepsydra, or ***water clock***, relied, as its name suggests, on water rather than sunshine. The water clock was invented in Babylon in around 1600 BCE. Unlike the sundial, this timekeeping device could be used on cloudy days—and at night. A water clock was a bowl with water in it and a small hole at the bottom, allowing the water to flow out at a steady rate. The drop in water level signaled the passage of time. Lines or markings inscribed inside the bowl indicated each passing hour.

But the water clock had a downside too. It could only be used in warm weather. In countries where temperatures dip during winter, the water in these clocks turned to ice. And that's why the Chinese came up with the idea of using mercury instead of water. While water freezes at 32°F (0°C), mercury freezes at -38°F (-38.9°C), making it far better at withstanding the cold.

A baboon adorns this model of an Egyptian water clock, now on display at the Metropolitan Museum of Art in New York City.
METROPOLITAN MUSEUM OF ART, GIFT OF J. PIERPONT MORGAN, 1917

The Origins of Clockwise

Clockwise refers to the direction that the hands of a clock move, which is to the right. *Counter-clockwise* refers to rotating to the left. But who decided that—and why? The answer has to do with ancient shadow clocks. Because Egypt, where shadow clocks originated, is located in the northern hemisphere, the shadow cast on the ground by a gnomon moves in an arc from left to right. That's why to this day, a clock's hands move in that direction. Had the shadow clock been invented in Australia, in the southern hemisphere, our clock hands, and the water in our toilet bowls, would move the other way.

RASULOVS/GETTY IMAGES

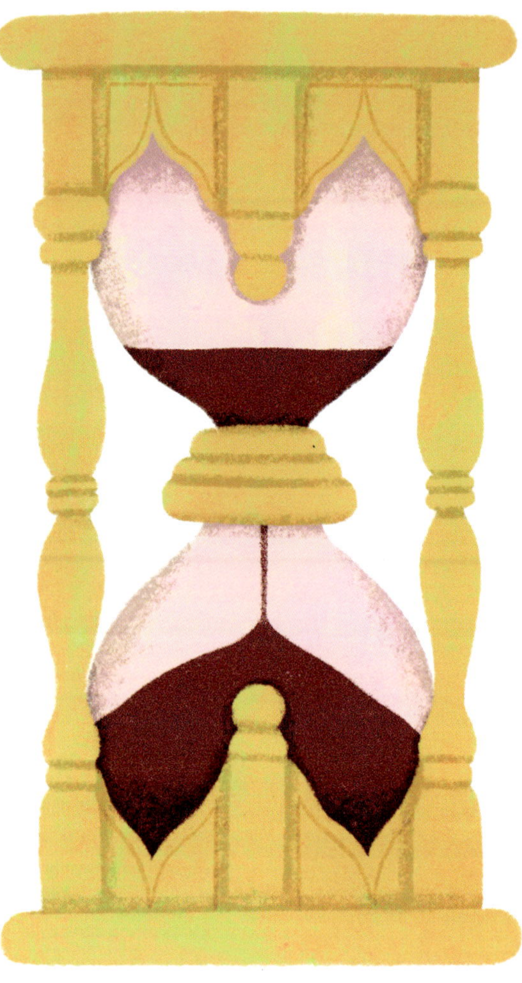

The Sands of Time

Hourglass | Chartres, France | Eighth century

The hourglass dates back to eighth-century Europe. This timekeeping device consists of two clear glass globes attached by a narrow neck. The narrow neck allows sand to flow from the upper to the lower globe. The hourglass, or sandglass, can be used to measure hours or minutes, depending on the amount of sand and the size of the neck connecting the globes. When used aboard a vessel along with the ship's log, it was known as a log glass. A log is an instrument that measures a ship's speed. The term dates from the early days of sailing, when sailors would throw a log of wood with a line attached to it from the rear of the ship. The line had regularly spaced knots in it, and by counting the number of knots that passed through their hands in a specified time (measured by an hourglass), sailors could calculate the ship's speed. Sailors recorded this information in their ships' *log*books, and from it they were able to calculate the distances their ships traveled. If the seas got rough, causing a lot of movement aboard ship, the hourglass, which was typically hung from the ceiling, kept working—unlike a water clock, which might overturn and spill its contents.

Ahoy, Matey!

Pirate ships used flags to send messages to enemy ships. These flags were made of sailcloth blackened with tar. One popular pirate ship flag featured an hourglass. Flying this flag warned other ships that their time was running out—and death was approaching. In our society the hourglass is a popular emoji used to indicate that time is nearly up. On Snapchat the hourglass emoji means your Snapstreak is coming to an end.

WIKIMEDIA COMMONS/PUBLIC DOMAIN

ROBAS/GETTY IMAGES

Moving Parts

Mechanical Clock
Bedfordshire, England 1283

The ***mechanical clock*** was invented toward the end of the 13th century. This clock had moving parts (hence the name mechanical), including a descending weight and gear wheels. Its most important part was its escapement, a mechanical linkage that regulates motion. The escapement causes the gears to move forward in a series of equal jumps. Because early mechanical clocks used weights, these clocks were big and heavy and almost impossible to move around.

Watchmaker Peter Henlein was from Nuremberg, Germany. His first watch was known as the Nuremberg egg because of its oval shape.
WIKIMEDIA COMMONS/CC BY-SA 4.0

The first weight-driven mechanical clock was installed in a church tower in England. The clock ensured that monks would not be late for daily prayers.

The ***mechanical watch*** first appeared in the early 16th century and was a sign of wealth. German locksmith Peter Henlein is believed to have created the first watch. Early watches were powered by a mainspring. Winding up the mainspring stored mechanical energy, which turned the clockwork gears and moved the hands of the watch. Mechanical watches such as the ones created by Henlein could keep time for up to 40 hours after winding.

All in the Family

Grandfather Clock
London, England 1670s

The ***grandfather clock*** has mechanical elements. Enclosed in a tall wooden case, it is powered by a ***pendulum***, or hanging weight, that swings back and forth. The first grandfather clock was made in the 1670s by British clockmaker William Clement. His invention was known as a floor clock or longcase clock. The term *grandfather clock* was first used in 1876, inspired by Henry Clay Work's popular song "Grandfather's Clock."

Early grandfather clocks were built six feet tall.
ALEKSANDR NAUMENKO/GETTY IMAGES

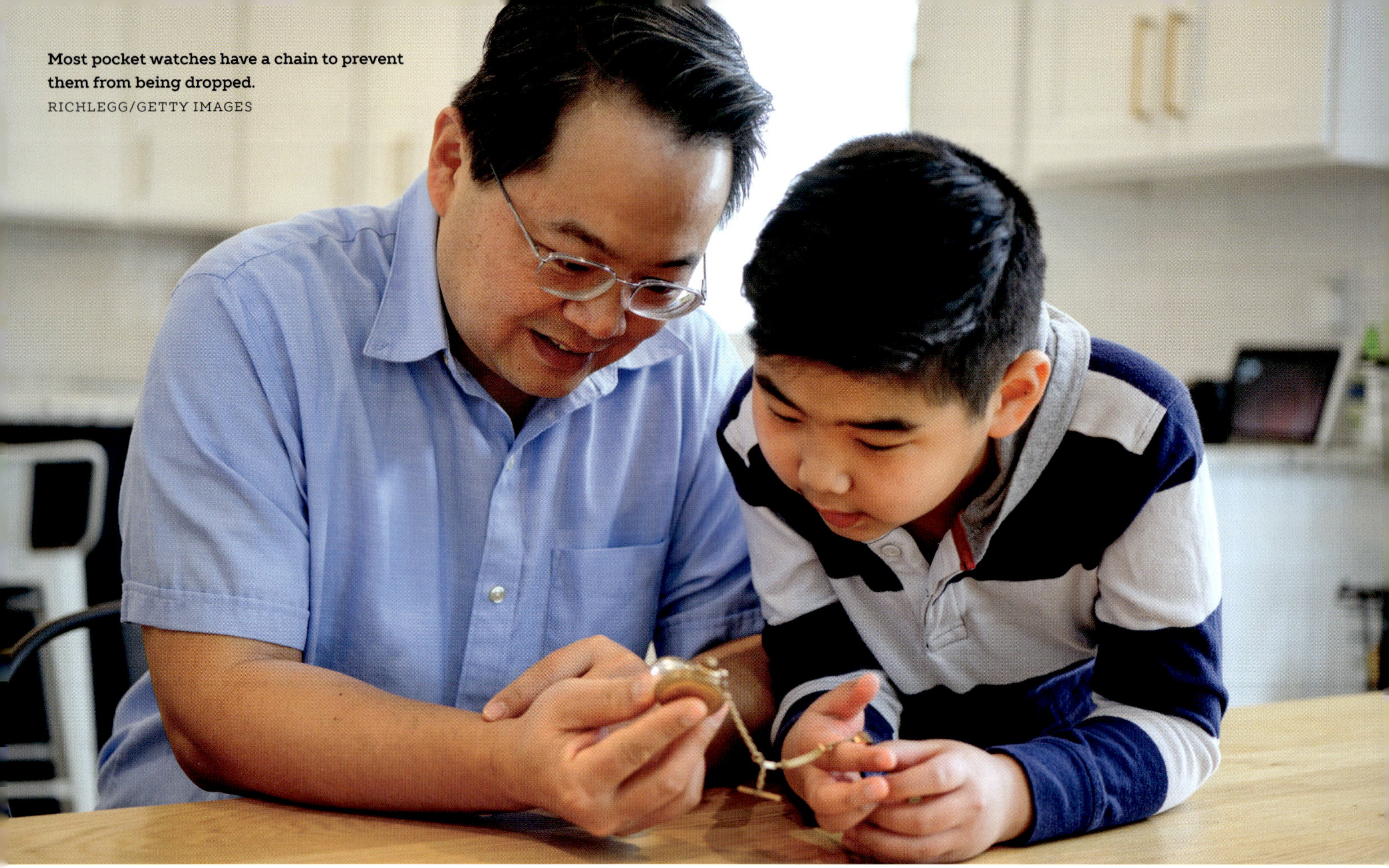

Most pocket watches have a chain to prevent them from being dropped.
RICHLEGG/GETTY IMAGES

"Oh dear! Oh dear! I shall be too late!"

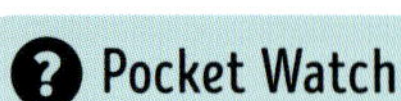

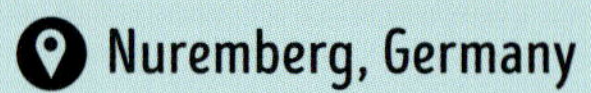

The White Rabbit in Lewis Carroll's beloved children's book *Alice's Adventures in Wonderland* checks the time on the watch he keeps in the pocket of his waistcoat. Pocket watches were introduced in the 1500s. They gained popularity around 1675, when King Charles II introduced a new fashion called the waistcoat. Once there were waistcoats, wealthy gentlemen began displaying their pocket watches. These watches were flat with glass-covered faces. By the mid-19th century, pocket watches had become far less expensive, so people who were not wealthy could afford to wear them too. Nowadays if you are looking for a waistcoat pocket watch, you should probably head to an antique store—or check out what's available on eBay.

"'The time has come,' the Walrus said, 'to talk of many things: Of shoes—and ships—and sealing-wax—of cabbages—and kings.'"

—**Lewis Carroll**, author

Powering Up

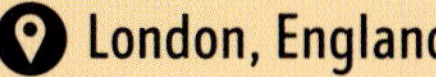

Electric Clock London, England

1814

British scientist Sir Francis Ronalds is believed to have invented the first ***electric clock***. The year was 1814, and Ronalds's clock was powered by a high-voltage battery. An electric impulse operated the clock's dials. The first ***quartz clock*** was invented in the United States in 1927. These clocks, which are also electric, use quartz crystal and remain popular today. Even an inexpensive quartz clock is fairly reliable, keeping time with an error of only about one second per day.

A Swiss-made electromechanical self-winding clock.
ANONIMSKI/WIKIMEDIA COMMONS/CC0

Most wristwatch batteries are made of silver oxide or lithium.
ANDREYPOPOV/GETTY IMAGES

Going Digital

Plato Clock

New York, United States  1904

Digital clocks that show the time in numerical digits make it super easy to tell what time it is. (The term *digital* refers to the display itself, not to the internal drive mechanism.) Digital clocks can be either mechanical or electronic. The earliest digital clock was invented back in 1883. A similar type of clock, called the Plato clock, caused a great sensation when it was exhibited in 1904 at the St. Louis World Fair. Shaped like a cylinder, the Plato clock used numbered cards that flipped to display the time. It wasn't until the 1970s, when LED displays were introduced, that digital clocks and wristwatches became popular.

A Timely Lesson

Most kids learn to tell time on an analog clock—a clock with a face and hands—when they are between five and seven years old. A time-telling lesson usually begins with learning about the hour hand on a clock, and the minute hand next. Though some people believe it's no longer necessary for kids to know how to tell time this way, it turns out that acquiring this skill has other benefits—it teaches basic math and helps kids grasp the concept of time.

a quarter past 3

a quarter to 4

Learning to tell time on an analog clock lets children practice fractions as well as skip-counting by fives (counting forward by five instead of one).
PETER DAZELEY/GETTY IMAGES

Sharing Is Caring

Quartz Watch | Tokyo, Japan | 1969

The world's first commercial quartz watch was introduced in 1969 by Seiko, a Japanese company. The watch contained a crystal oscillator that vibrated at a steady rhythm when voltage was applied to it. Because Seiko realized the importance of accurate timekeeping, it openly shared its patent for this invention with other watchmaking companies. Seiko was founded by Kintaro Hattori, who in 1881, at the age of 21, opened a shop in Tokyo that sold and repaired watches and clocks. In 1923, after the Great Kantō Earthquake struck Tokyo, Hattori ran a newspaper ad offering to replace any Seiko watch or clock damaged during the earthquake.

When he first visited a clock shop at the age of 13, Kintaro Hattori decided he wanted to become a clockmaker.

(TOP) MUSEUMSFOTO/WIKIMEDIA COMMONS/ CC BY-SA 3.0; (BOTTOM) WIKIMEDIA COMMONS/ PUBLIC DOMAIN

Seeing Is Believing

Time Blindness  1997

Seeing the time on a digital display makes telling time quick and easy. One peek at the top right of my computer screen, and I know exactly what time it is. But it turns out that using an old-fashioned analog clock has important benefits—especially when it comes to time management. Research indicates that people who use clocks with hands and dials have a more concrete, visual sense of the passage of time than those who rely on digital timekeeping devices. Say, for example, your digital clock tells you it is 7:45 in the morning—you may feel there is still time to do a few things before you leave to catch the eight o'clock bus. But if you see the hands on the clock approaching 8:00, you are more likely to head out the door. Psychologists who work with kids and adults with ADHD recommend that they keep an analog clock on their desks. Scientists found that analog clocks help prevent a condition sometimes referred to as ***time blindness***, a term coined in 1997—in which people lose awareness of the passage of time and may end up missing that 8:00 a.m. bus!

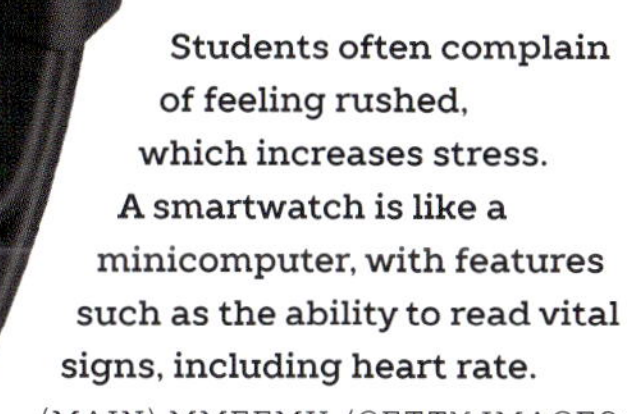

Students often complain of feeling rushed, which increases stress. A smartwatch is like a minicomputer, with features such as the ability to read vital signs, including heart rate.

(MAIN) MMEEMIL/GETTY IMAGES; (INSET) DOOMU/GETTY IMAGES

A satellite in space relays communications from one place on Earth to another.
YUICHIRO CHINO/GETTY IMAGES

Precisely on Time

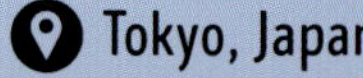

If you're looking for the most accurate time possible, you'll need an atomic clock. These clocks measure time by monitoring the ***resonant frequency*** of atoms. Most atomic clocks use cesium atoms, which oscillate at a set and reliable number of cycles per second. And as you learned in chapter 2, these atomic clocks keep time with an error of only one second in 300 million years. GPS solar watches were introduced in 2012. These watches use signals from GPS satellites that orbit Earth to adjust time and date. Each satellite contains many atomic clocks.

Like Clockwork

Pendulum, digital, quartz and atomic clocks have more in common than you might expect. They all measure time by counting the ticks of a resonator, a device that vibrates, generating a frequency. The pendulum is the resonator in a pendulum clock; its gears count each swing of the pendulum. Just as atomic clocks rely on atoms to provide resonance, digital clocks measure time by using the oscillations of electrical circuits, and quartz crystal acts as the resonator for quartz clocks.

PETER DAZELEY/GETTY IMAGES

George Vernon Hudson

WIKIMEDIA COMMONS/PUBLIC DOMAIN

Spring Forward, Fall Back

Daylight saving time (DST) is used in 70 countries and affects a billion people a year. In the parts of Canada and the United States that observe DST, the clock jumps ahead an hour on the second Sunday of March (when DST begins) and falls back an hour on the first Sunday of November (when DST comes to an end). Germany was the first country to adopt DST, as a way of conserving coal during World War I. Ever since then people have been arguing about DST. Those who are opposed point to—among other things—the disruption in sleep patterns, especially in adolescents who like to stay up late and sleep in the next day. New Zealand entomologist George Vernon Hudson is credited with suggesting DST back in 1895. Hudson wanted more daylight hours so he could hunt for insects. But the idea behind DST goes back to the days of the water clock. In Roman times, water clocks used different scales for different times of year in keeping with the rhythm of the sun.

Digging Up the Past

Expo 1970 Time Capsule

Osaka, Japan  **6970**

Back in 1970, to celebrate Expo '70, held in Osaka, Japan, the Japanese watchmaking company Seiko partnered with a company, which later became Panasonic, to produce two plutonium clocks that were buried in an Osaka park. They used plutonium because it is an element that degrades super slowly and at a uniform speed. Each clock was part of a time capsule containing more than 2,000 objects. The first capsule was opened in 2000 and then closed back up. It will be reopened every 100 years. Those who are present in 2100, the next time the first capsule is opened, will gain a better understanding of what life was like in 1970. The second capsule with the second clock will stay buried for 5,000 years, providing our descendants with the opportunity to learn about the past.

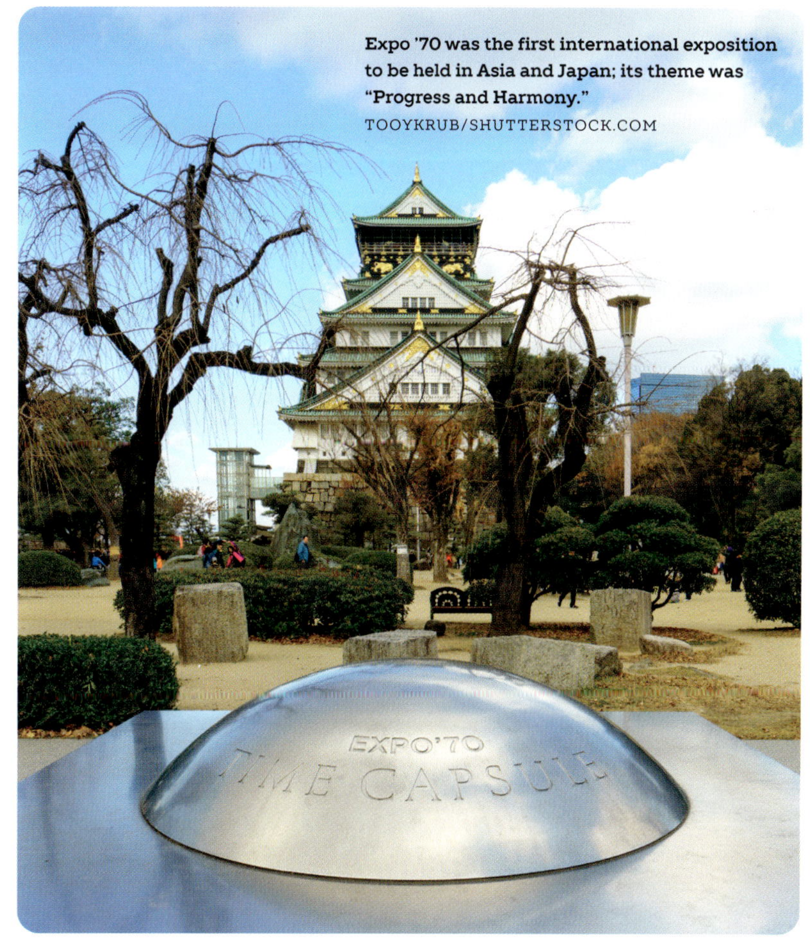

Expo '70 was the first international exposition to be held in Asia and Japan; its theme was "Progress and Harmony."
TOOYKRUB/SHUTTERSTOCK.COM

1796
Phrenology
4TH CENTURY
Saint Augustine
of Hippo
TODAY
Jet-lag apps
2017
Nobel Prize for studies
on circadian rhythms

FOUR

IT'S WHAT'S INSIDE THAT COUNTS

There's only a few more days to go until the end of the school year. You're looking forward to sleeping in, hanging out with your friends and taking that long-awaited camping trip with your family. But time seems to stand still. It feels like those last days in class drag on for a month. On the other hand you remember how fast last summer seemed to fly by. Does time actually slow down or speed up in our bodies depending on what's going on in our lives? Do we have an internal clock that can tell time, or do humans run based on what's happening in nature? It turns out our brain is, in fact, a master timekeeper, with multiple different clocks that keep track of all the systems in our bodies.

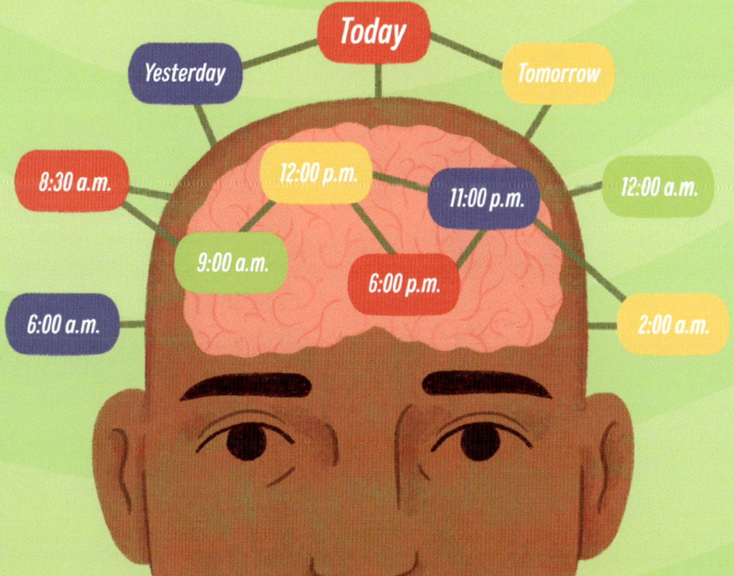

Today we know that the human brain measures time both in a biological way *and* through how we experience events.
SDI PRODUCTIONS/GETTY IMAGES

It's in My Head

Saint Augustine of Hippo | Ancient Rome | 354–430

In the fourth century Saint Augustine of Hippo was one of the first people to think of time as something that exists *inside* the human mind. He was a Christian ***theologian*** and philosopher, and the patron saint of brewers (but that's another story). In Book XI of his work *Confessions*, he writes about the past, present and future, and asks how we can understand the idea of time passing if we only truly exist in the present. "It is within my mind, then, that I measure time," he concluded. In a sense he wasn't wrong, but it would be hundreds of years later before scientists could actually study the brain itself to prove he was right.

"Change will not come if we wait for some other person or some other time."

—**Barack Obama**, former US president

Big Bumps

If people couldn't look inside the brain to understand in any meaningful way how the body and mind told time, they decided to focus on the outside of the head instead. They came up with some far-fetched ideas to explain how time worked! In 1796 Franz Joseph Gall, a German physician, invented phrenology. Phrenologists divided the human skull into 27 zones (later it grew to 35 zones) representing different abilities and character traits, including one for measuring time. Today phrenology is regarded as a pseudoscience, which means the ideas have no basis in scientific fact.

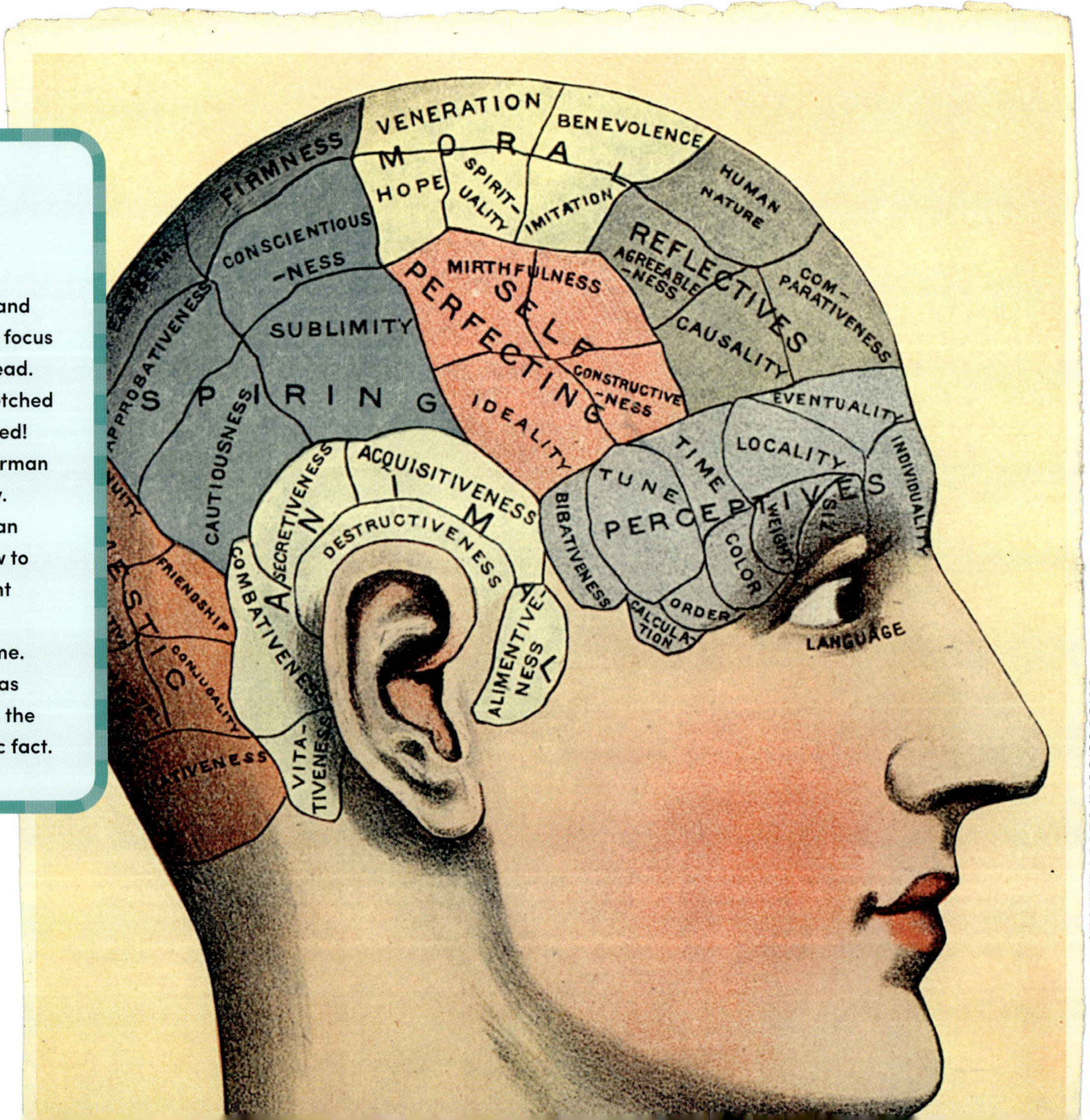

PHOTOS.COM/GETTY IMAGES

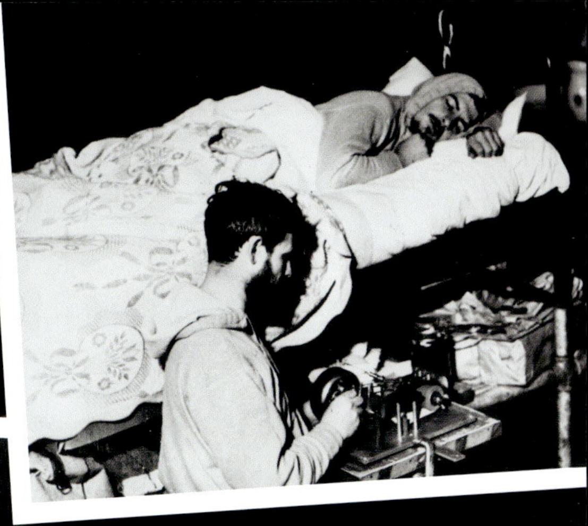

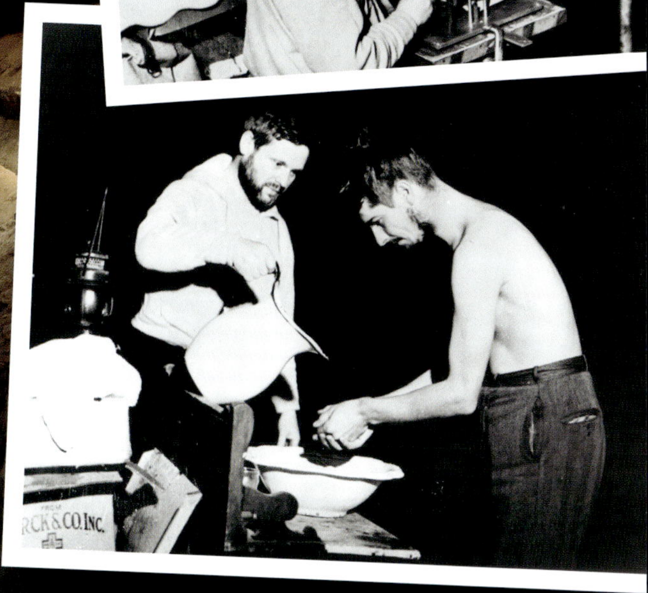

Cave Dwelling

Mammoth Cave Experiment | Kentucky, United States | 1938

At the time, Nathaniel Kleitman's research at Mammoth Cave in Kentucky was seen as an interesting experiment. In reality, it helped kick off the science of sleep.
(LEFT) POSNOV/GETTY IMAGES; (RIGHT) HANNA HOLBORN GRAY SPECIAL COLLECTIONS RESEARCH CENTER, UNIVERSITY OF CHICAGO LIBRARY

Plants, insects and animals live, eat, mate and sleep based on natural cycles and the regular patterns of daylight and darkness in nature (we'll talk more about this later). These are called ***circadian rhythms***. Humans live by these rhythms too. That's why we sleep when it's dark and wake up when the sun comes out. Researchers wanted to know whether these rhythms only worked in response to nature or whether there might be some other timekeeper at work inside the human body. In 1938 Nathaniel Kleitman, a sleep researcher at the University of Chicago, decided to test this theory by finding a "timeless" environment, somewhere without natural light and dark and all the other cues we typically use to tell what time it is. So along with one of his students, he lived in Mammoth Cave in Kentucky for 32 days.

It was the perfect place to test this theory because it was always dark in the cave and the temperature never changed—it stayed a steady 54°F (12°C) day and night. The two researchers experimented with the standard 24-hour cycle and used an alarm and electric lights to tell them when to eat, when to go to bed and when to wake up. In the end their daily patterns of sleeping and waking didn't change that much—they slept about the same number of hours as they would at home and woke up at roughly the same time. Kleitman's study was one of the first to show that the human body generally maintains a 24-hour cycle even without any natural cues like sunlight.

The Early Bird Gets the Worm

Do you like staying up late and sleeping in? Then you're probably a night owl. If you like going to sleep early and jumping out of bed first thing in the morning, then you're an early bird, or "lark." Scientists have found that owls and larks (and everything in between) exist because everyone's circadian rhythm is slightly different. You may have noticed that your sleep/wake cycles have changed throughout your life—young children are typically larks and become more like owls once they hit their teens. Turn off that alarm clock!

The Graveyard Shift

Firefighters, nurses, bakers and truck drivers all have jobs that require ***shift work***. If your job means you work overnight instead of during the day for months or even years in a row, it can be bad for your health. A study from the University of Missouri School of Medicine discovered that the cells in your body don't adapt to the graveyard shift as fast as your brain does, especially if you shift back to a normal schedule on the weekends when you're not working. That creates something called circadian misalignment (confusion between cells and the brain) and can lead to higher rates of depression, anxiety, heart attacks, stroke and cancer.

On average, shift workers get around 10 hours less sleep per week than people who work during the day.
ER PRODUCTIONS LIMITED/GETTY IMAGES

You're Feeling Sleepy

Nobel Prize in Physiology and Medicine, for Studies of Circadian Rhythms

Jeffrey C. Hall, Michael Rosbash and Michael W. Young  2017

Today scientists know that the master timekeeper of the circadian system in the human brain is the ***suprachiasmatic nucleus (SCN)***, found in the ***hypothalamus***, and that its rhythms are based on both external and internal factors. That means we usually—if we're not living in a cave—go to sleep at night because it's dark outside but also because other internal clocks tell our bodies to start producing melatonin, the sleep hormone. When melatonin is released, our bodies move from an active phase to a resting phase.

But our circadian rhythms don't just help us with day and night. They also regulate other biological processes in our bodies, including our temperature, appetite and mood. Even though scientists knew these internal clocks existed, they didn't know how they worked. In 2017 three American scientists, Jeffrey C. Hall, Michael Rosbash and Michael W. Young, received the Nobel Prize for their decades of work on our internal biological clocks—they helped figure out what made them tick all the way to the cellular level. Today wearable technologies like smartwatches are helping scientists understand more about circadian health in the human body, by monitoring sleep habits, for example.

Electronic devices like phones or smartwatches can get in the way of a good night's sleep. Your brain thinks the blue light they emit is daylight and keeps you awake.
OSCAR WONG/GETTY IMAGES

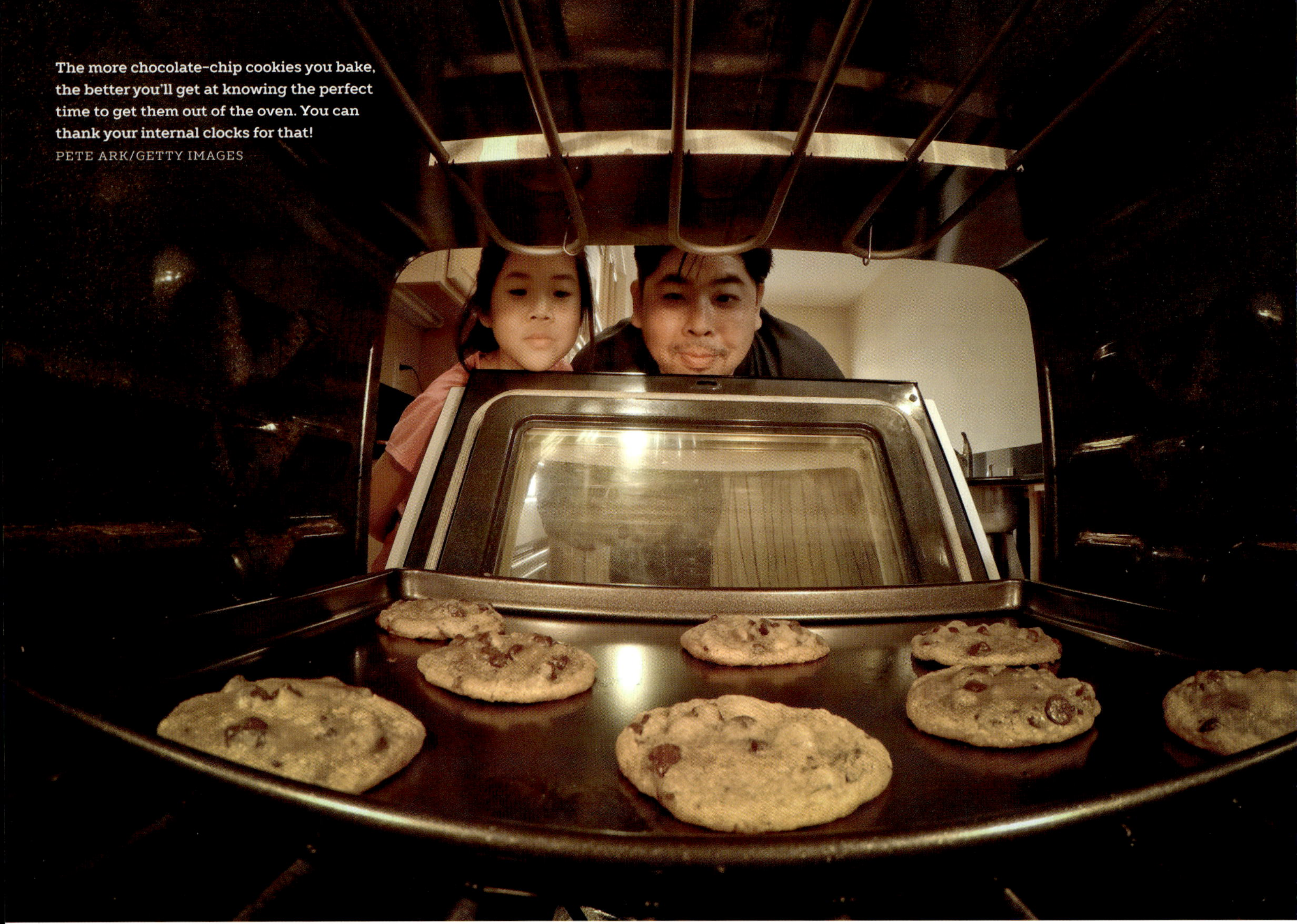

The more chocolate-chip cookies you bake, the better you'll get at knowing the perfect time to get them out of the oven. You can thank your internal clocks for that!
PETE ARK/GETTY IMAGES

Ticking Clocks

Time Cells | University of Texas Southwestern, United States | 2020

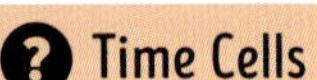

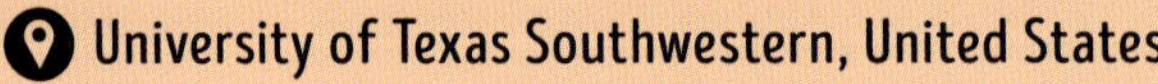

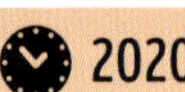

Have you ever walked into the kitchen just as the timer beeps on the oven to tell you the chocolate-chip cookies are ready? How did you know to walk in right at that moment? Was it just a coincidence, or did your brain know how much time it would take them to bake?

As you just learned, circadian rhythms are only one of the ways our brains tell time. Scientists now know that we have multiple mental clocks keeping track of time in our bodies, and they are found in different areas of the brain, from the ***hippocampus*** to the ***striatum***. Time cells are responsible for recording the passage of time—the start and end of the memories we make—from minutes all the way down to the millisecond. They do that by firing at regular moments during an experience. If you've made cookies before, your time cells have stamped in your memory how long it took for them to bake, so you have a sense of when to check on them.

In a 2020 study scientists observed these time cells at work when they studied a group of patients waiting for surgery for epilepsy. The patients were shown a set of words in a particular order. After running through the set multiple times, the researchers would stop and ask the patients to remember which came next. Researchers found that time cells had made a stamp of whatever the person was seeing in a particular moment. When they were asked to remember what came next, even if the words stopped, the time cells fired in the same order.

Neuroscientists are still learning how all the different mental clocks in our brains work and how they work together. But you can thank your time cells when you get that nagging feeling that it's time to get out of the shower and get ready for school.

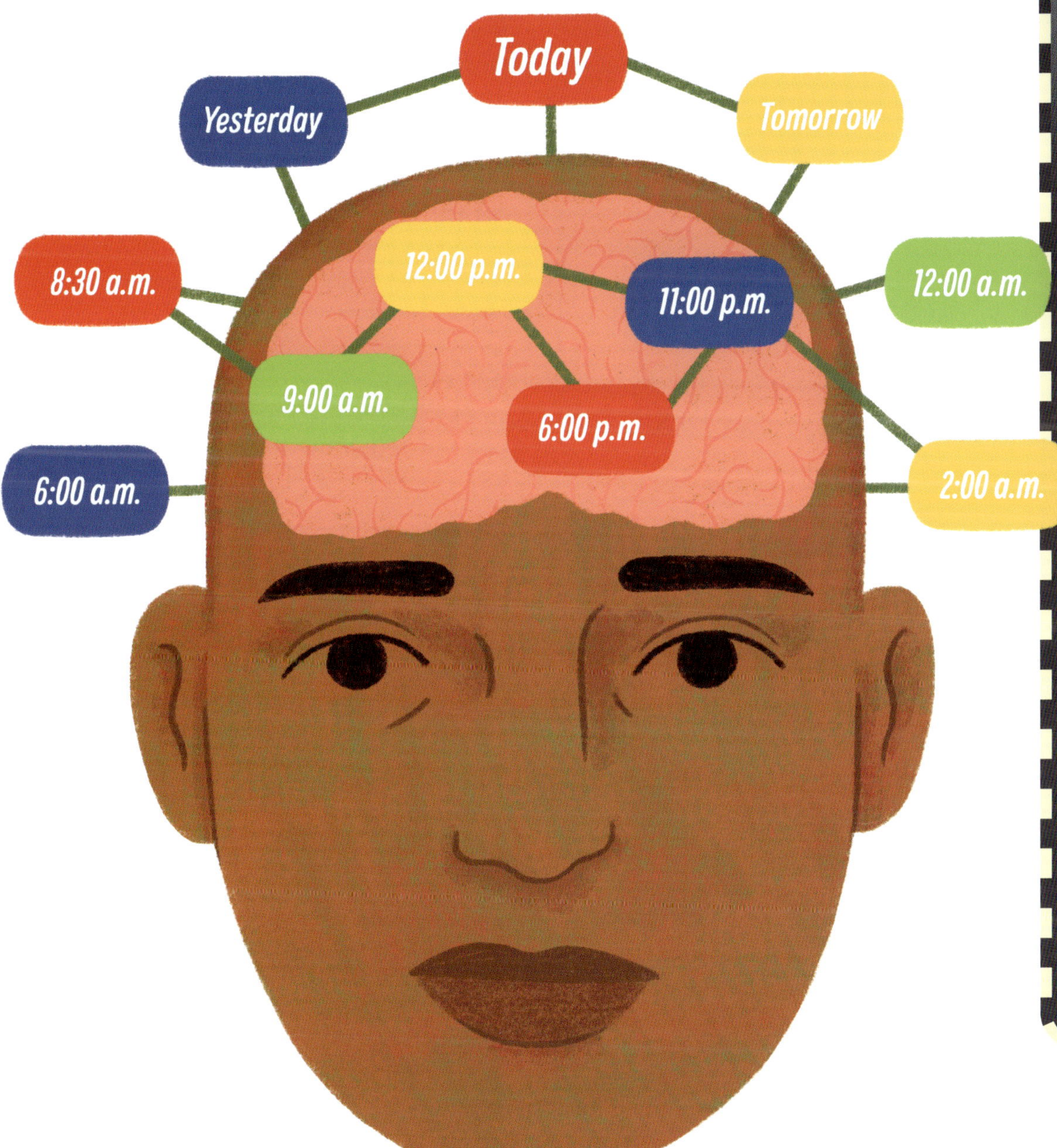

Lagging Behind

Formula One drivers travel to as many as 20 countries over their nine-month racing season. That means they cross multiple time zones between races. Jet lag can seriously affect their performance. It's a disorder that can cause a temporary disruption of their body's normal circadian rhythms. Jet lag can affect anyone, but athletes who regularly travel all over the world for competitions and have to be at their best when they arrive need a strategy for how they're going to manage the time change long before they get on a plane. Carlos Sainz is a Formula One driver. He has a jet-lag plan that depends on caffeine, light exposure and even adjusting his sleep to the time zone he's traveling to days in advance of getting on the plane. And yes, there's an app for that. The Timeshifter app helps you manage your jet lag and tells you when it's time for bed.

EV. SAFRONOV/SHUTTERSTOCK.COM

Slow Down or Speed Up?

You're probably familiar with the saying *Time flies when you're having fun*. We've all felt this way, and there are several reasons why our "mind" time differs from actual clock time. One has to do with our emotional state. When we're happily involved in an activity we enjoy, like playing a sport we love or going to a friend's birthday party, our brains release more dopamine, a chemical that makes the brain think that less time has passed than actually has. On the other hand, if we're bored or waiting for something to happen, and we're not having fun, less dopamine is released, and time seems to slow down.

As people get older they often say that time seems to be flying by. Although there's no consensus on exactly why this is the case, there are several theories. First off, it's a numbers game. When you're 10, one year is 10 percent of your life, giving it more weight than when you're 100 and a year represents just 1 percent of your life.

According to Adrian Bejan, a professor at Duke University, there's also a relationship between how fast your brain is processing new images and your perception of time. When you're young and learning lots of new things, your brain is processing many images to make memories, and that can actually make it feel like time is passing slowly. As you get older the rate at which your brain processes new images and experiences tends to slow down, giving the sense that time has passed quickly. "There's an inversely proportional relationship between stimuli processing and the sense of time speeding by," Bejan says.

Researcher Ricardo Correia, from the University of Turku in Finland, examined how people's perception of time changed depending on whether they were in an urban or a natural environment. He found that being in nature slows time down in the brain, making it seem longer than it does when we're, say, walking down a busy city street. It can be good for our health to take a break from clock time every now and then! So think about that the next time you're taking a walk in the woods.

ARVYDAS LAKACAUSKAS/GETTY IMAGES

A magic potion to turn back the clock isn't coming anytime soon, but older people can stay mentally and physically healthy for longer by trying a new sport, something that engages the mind and the body.
YOSHIYOSHI HIROKAWA/GETTY IMAGES

Turn Back the Clock

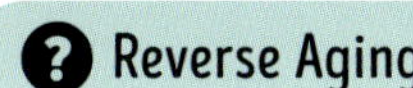 Reverse Aging 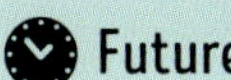 Future

Whether time is passing slowly or quickly for you right now, one thing is certain—you're getting older every day. But what if there were a magic potion that could turn back the clock and reverse time? There aren't many of us who wouldn't jump at the chance for even one drop of being a few years younger again. It turns out that the idea might not be as far-fetched as you think.

In 2023 a Harvard Medical School study led by David Sinclair was able to speed up and then reverse aging in mice. In the lab Sinclair's team artificially aged young mice by making breaks in their DNA. Within a few weeks the mice had gray hair and acted older, showing signs of frailty. The scientists then used gene therapy to reverse the changes they had caused in the DNA and made the mice young again. The next step for Sinclair and his team is to find out if a similar process could work in humans. That's a few years down the road, but for now the hope is that this research could be used to study how to prevent specific age-related conditions such as eye, heart and Alzheimer's diseases.

Time for Something New

One reason older people are encouraged to pick up new hobbies, like playing an instrument or learning to paint, is to slow the apparent passing of time—and doing so has the added benefit of helping to keep your brain healthy.

4TH CENTURY BCE
The tamarind tree
1860
Monarch butterfly migration
2018
Animal timing cells
FUTURE
Chronoculture
FUTURE
Tree rings

FIVE

CAN YOUR DOG—OR YOUR HOUSEPLANT—TELL TIME?

You're sitting in the kitchen waiting for dinner. You look at the time on the stove. It says six o'clock. Right on cue your dog walks over to their food dish and looks at you with those sad puppy-dog eyes. You know what they're trying to say. *Feed me, feed me.* How did your dog know it was six o'clock? Can your dog tell time?

It turns out they can—in a manner of speaking. They don't use watches or clocks like humans, but they have their own internal systems to tell time. And our pets aren't the only ones with this special power. Examples of timekeeping can be found everywhere in nature—in plants and fungi and in insects, birds and other wild animals. This ability doesn't just help them survive, it helps them adapt to a changing climate. And it means we can learn from them too.

The Svalbard Ptarmigan

Most animals have a 24-hour clock that relies on the sun to help them figure out when it's night and when it's day and, therefore, when it's time to eat, sleep, hunt or find a mate. But the high Arctic has summer days without any darkness and winter days without any sunlight. So how do animals living there keep time? Researchers at the University of Tromso in Norway studied the Svalbard ptarmigan, the world's northernmost resident bird species. They found that the ptarmigan didn't have daily circadian rhythms like birds and animals living farther south. They've adapted to their habitats by having a seasonal rhythm instead of a daily one. Their light-sensitive internal clock tells them when it's spring—and so time to start looking for a mate.

BUBLIKPOLINA/GETTY IMAGES

The Tamarind Tree

Androsthenes

Fourth century BCE

By examining nature over thousands of years, humans observed that plants and animals lived their lives based on patterns of daylight and darkness. In the fourth century BCE, Androsthenes, one of Alexander the Great's sea captains, noticed how the leaves of a tamarind tree opened and closed at the same time every day. This was the first written observation of a circadian rhythm in nature. Almost every organism on the planet has this internal clock, not just animals (including humans) but also plants, fungi and even some bacteria.

A Dark Room

Jean-Jacques d'Ortous de Mairan

1729

For hundreds of years it was thought that these 24-hour internal cycles only happened in response to environmental factors like sunlight. For example, the tamarind tree's leaves opened when the sun was out and closed at night when it was dark. But in 1729 French scientist Jean-Jacques d'Ortous de Mairan put a *Mimosa pudica* plant in a dark room for a few days. He saw that its leaves opened and closed in a regular cycle without exposure to any light. That meant the plant's circadian rhythm also depended on some other internal clock that could predict when it should be light and dark, instead of just reacting when the sun rose and set. It turns out he was right.

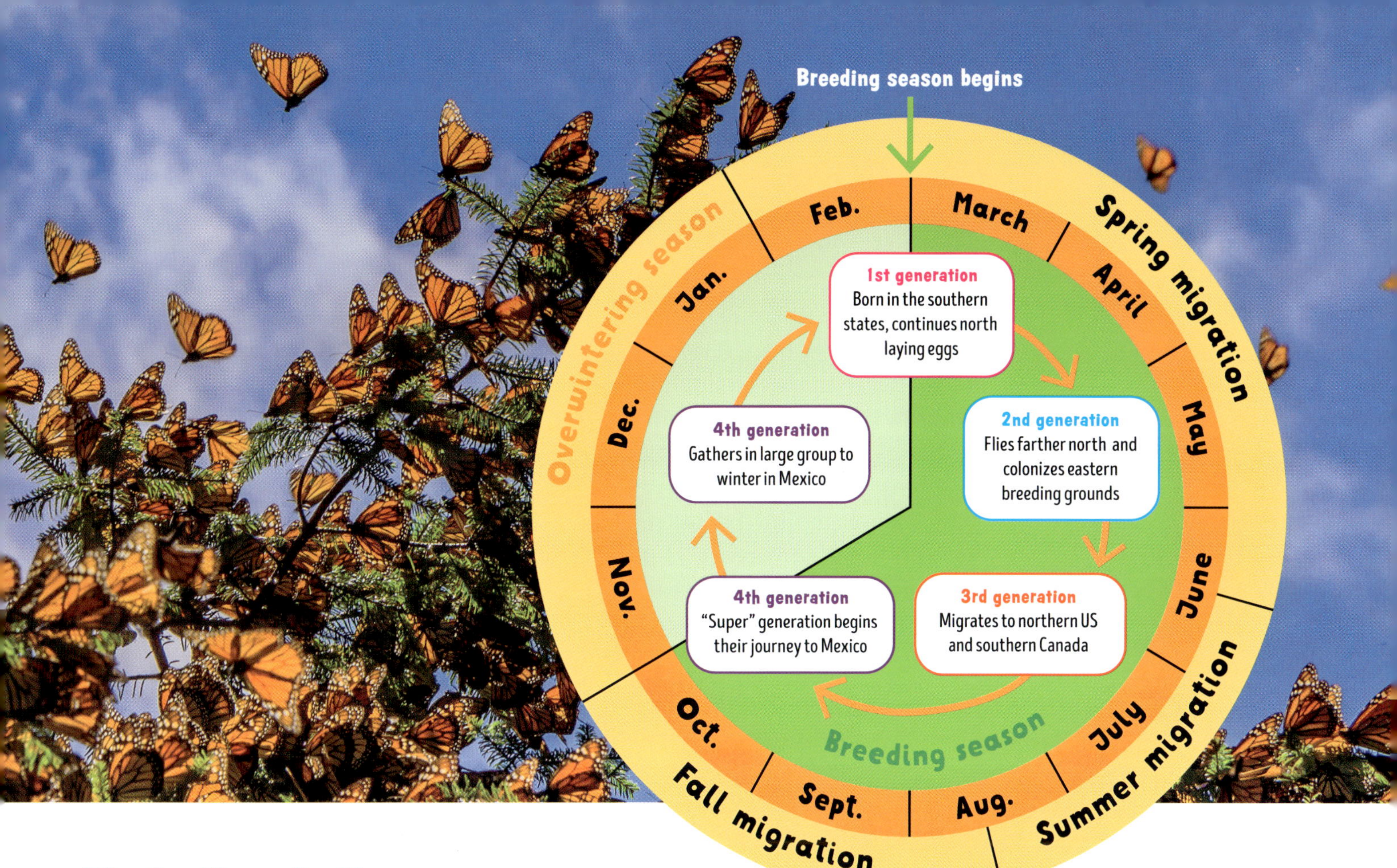

Fly to Your Left

Monarch Butterfly Migration | Mexico to Canada | 

Monarch butterflies have one of the greatest migrations on Earth. Every year at the same time, millions of monarchs make an almost 2,500-mile (4,000-kilometer) migration from their winter homes in Mexico to their summer breeding grounds in the northern United States and southern Canada. The migration was first documented in 1860, but scientists think it could have been happening for as long as one million years. It can take up to four butterfly generations to make the round trip. That means a grandparent starts the northward journey and their great-grandchild finishes it back in Mexico. But how do they know which direction to go, and when? And how do they arrive at the exact same spot every year?

Steven Reppert and his team at the University of Massachusetts discovered that they do it through a combination of their internal clock (circadian rhythm) and a brain compass that tracks where the sun is in the sky. But the sun doesn't stay still—it moves throughout the day, so the researchers knew there had to be something else helping the later generations of butterflies keep track of time as they navigated south. The study revealed that the "clock" is in their antennae. If the sun is close to the horizon, these clocks tell the butterfly whether it's rising or setting and whether it's in the east or the west. "If the sun is in the east, for example, the butterfly flies with the sun on its left to go south," Reppert says.

Monarch butterflies can travel up to 100 miles (160 kilometers) a day as they migrate between Mexico and and the northern United States and southern Canada.

(MAIN) JHVEPHOTO/GETTY IMAGES; (INSET) ADAPTED FROM NPS.GOV/SUBJECTS/POLLINATORS/MIGRATINGMONARCHS.HTM. NPS GRAPHIC/S. SPARHAWK/PUBLIC DOMAIN

"Time spent with cats is never wasted."

—Colette, French author

MARTINE SEVERIN/GETTY IMAGES

I'm Waiting

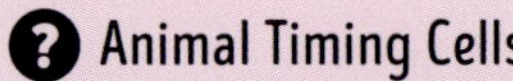

Animal Timing Cells | Northwestern University, United States | 2018

Dogs are usually excited to see their owner when they get home at the end of the day. But researchers at the Swedish University of Agricultural Sciences found that a dog's level of excitement changed depending on how long the owner was gone. And you guessed it. The longer they were gone, the more tail wagging, lip licking and body shaking happened when the owner and their dog were reunited. Did that mean the dog knew whether they were alone for 10 minutes or a few hours?

A study from Northwestern University found that animals have a set of ***neurons*** in their brains that turn on like a clock when they're waiting for something, like you coming home at the end of the day. And yes, that means a dog knows when it's time for dinner. To test this the researchers had a mouse run on a treadmill in a virtual-reality space. It would run to a door, wait six seconds for the door to open and get a reward before continuing down the track. Then the researchers made the door invisible. The mouse still ran to the same space, waited six seconds and moved on. The mouse was judging time to sense when the "door" would open. When researchers looked at its brain, they could see what they called timing cells, similar to those found in human brains, turning on.

According to researchers, the discovery of timing cells in the brains of animals means that your dog may know that it took you longer to get home from school today than it did yesterday.
JENA ARDELL/GETTY IMAGES

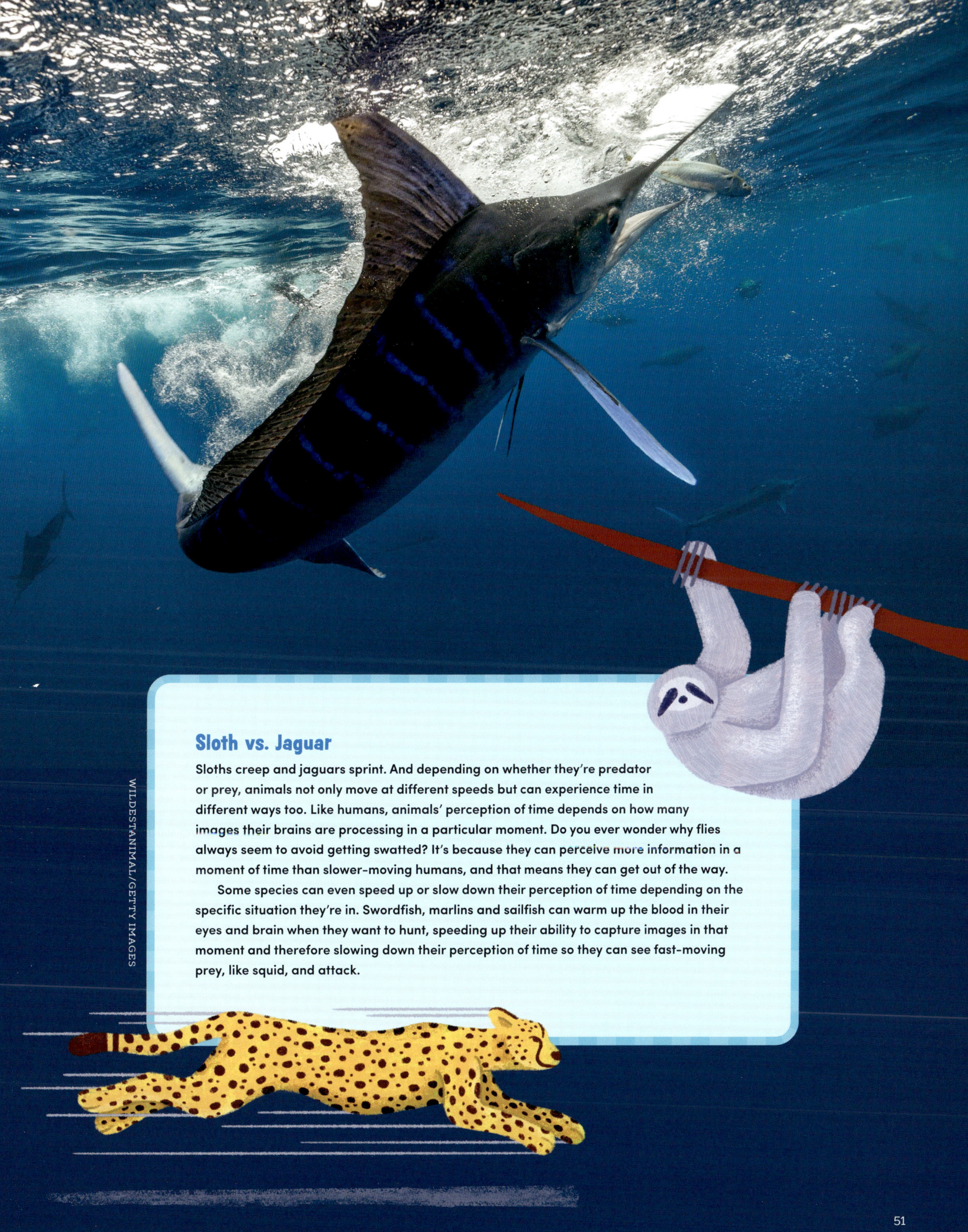

WILDESTANIMAL/GETTY IMAGES

Sloth vs. Jaguar

Sloths creep and jaguars sprint. And depending on whether they're predator or prey, animals not only move at different speeds but can experience time in different ways too. Like humans, animals' perception of time depends on how many images their brains are processing in a particular moment. Do you ever wonder why flies always seem to avoid getting swatted? It's because they can perceive more information in a moment of time than slower-moving humans, and that means they can get out of the way.

Some species can even speed up or slow down their perception of time depending on the specific situation they're in. Swordfish, marlins and sailfish can warm up the blood in their eyes and brain when they want to hunt, speeding up their ability to capture images in that moment and therefore slowing down their perception of time so they can see fast-moving prey, like squid, and attack.

The badlands of Dinosaur Provincial Park in Alberta were formed 75 million years ago during the late Cretaceous period. The area contains layers of sandstone and mudstone that are perfect for preserving dinosaur fossils.
SL_PHOTOGRAPHY/GETTY IMAGES

Geologic Time

Geologists are scientists who study how Earth was formed and what it's made of. They've divided the five billion years of the planet's history into very long time periods from its creation to today:

Eons	These are the longest periods in geological time and measure about 1 billion years each. There are four eons: the Hadean, the Archean, the Proterozoic and the Phanerozoic, the eon we're in today.
Eras	These are the second-longest spans of geological time. There are 10 eras. We're in the Cenozoic era, which started 66 million years ago. Eras are marked by changes in the ***fossil record***.
Periods	A period lasts tens of millions of years. They measure different types of life on the planet at a particular time. For example, dinosaurs went extinct at the end of the Cretaceous period, 65 million years ago.
Epochs	These are the shortest measure of geological time and measure millions of years. We're currently in the Holocene epoch.

Happy Birthday

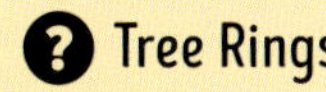 Tree Rings  Future

Trees make a ring for every year they grow, so if you count the rings, you'll know how old the tree is. They're a bit like birthday candles that way. If you look at the rings closely, you'll see that some are wider and some are thinner. That's because in warm, wet years they grow a lot, so the rings are wider, and in cold, dry years they grow less, so the rings are thinner. The size and type of ring can show whether there were floods, droughts and even fires in any given year. That means the rings can tell us a lot about what was happening in nature at a specific moment in time. They provide a climate history of an area for hundreds, and in the case of the oldest trees in the world, bristlecone pines, thousands of years. Today researchers are using that long timeline to help predict future climate events like droughts and wildfires caused by climate change. These predictions give people an idea of where extreme events might happen and how they can prepare.

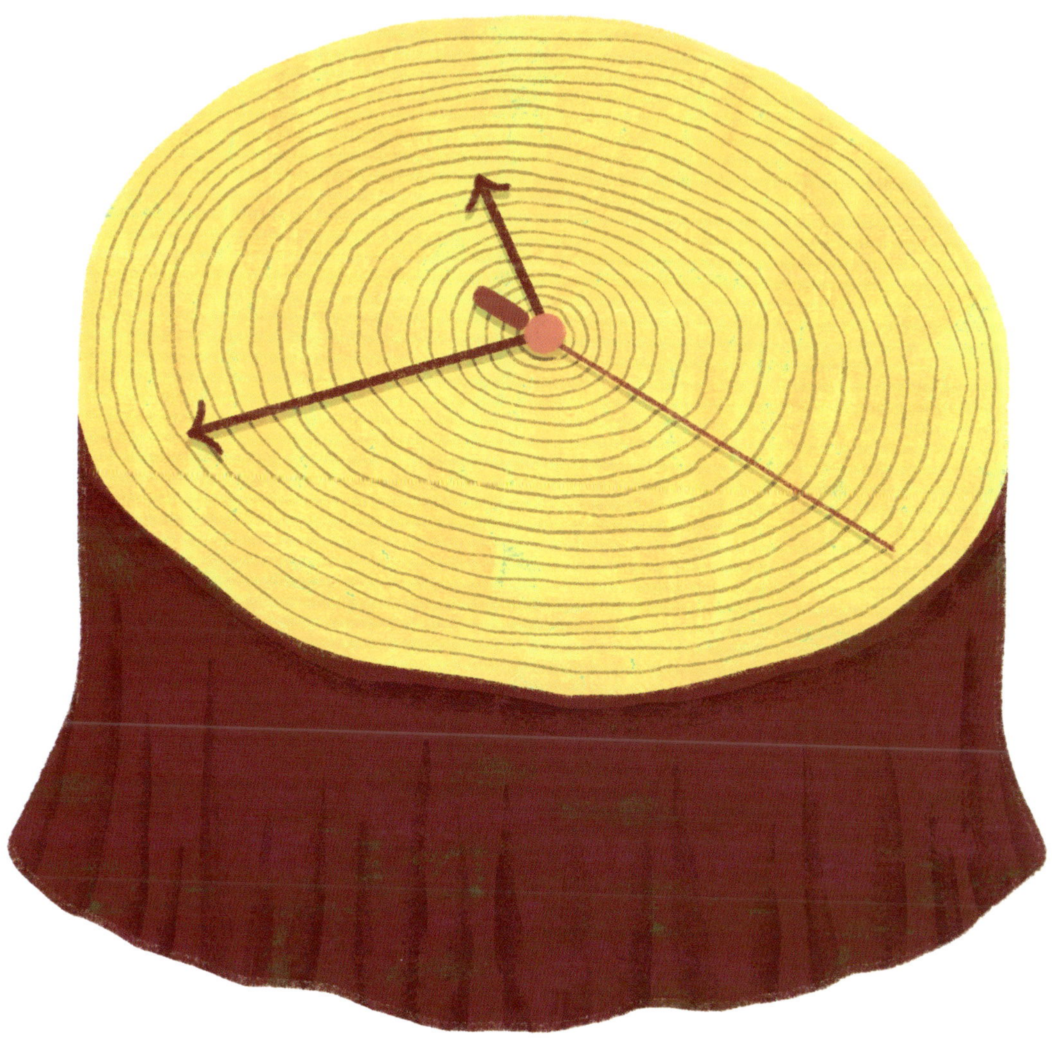

Giant sequoias, like this one in Kings Canyon National Park in California, can live for more than 3,000 years. That's a lot of birthdays!

YENWEN/GETTY IMAGES

Lettuce and Tomatoes for Everyone

Chronoculture 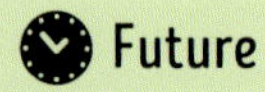 Future

Research shows that fruit and vegetable plants like lettuce, zucchini, carrots and blueberries have an internal clock that responds to light or darkness, just like humans do.
AEGEANBLUE/GETTY IMAGES

Plants do a great job of managing their time. Most flowers are open and ready for pollination when the sun is out, and they close up shop when it's dark so they have time to grow and develop. Researchers at the University of Cambridge say that understanding and using this natural cycle might be one of the solutions to food insecurity in the future. In one study they discovered that plants grow much better when their internal clock matches the environment they're growing in. So if farmers selected plants based on those circadian rhythms, it would mean they knew the ideal time to plant, water and protect their crops from pests with herbicides and pesticides.

This way of farming is known as ***chronoculture***, and it could also be helpful for indoor vertical farming, which is a sustainable way to use less land to grow more crops. In vertical farms plants are grown stacked one on top of the other in a controlled environment. The farmers decide when to water the plants, the ideal temperature the farm should be at, how much light the plants need and when they need it. By matching a plant's internal clock with the best conditions, they could produce even more lettuce or tomatoes. And all of this means more food for a hungry planet.

In a vertical farm, light, temperature and humidity can be controlled to match a crop's internal clock.
SERGEY MIRONOV

It's My Turn

Even though most plants have a 24-hour clock, they don't all open and close their flowers at the same time. Squash and pumpkins are early risers. Their flowers open first thing in the morning. Evening primrose blooms in the evening and closes by lunchtime the next day. And the moonflower—you guessed it—blooms in the moonlight. It's all to take advantage of pollinators and ensure that the plants don't compete with each other to attract insects.

2ND CENTURY
Siestas
TO-DO
1982
Time sickness
1986
The slow movement
PAST, PRESENT AND FUTURE
Kinship time

SIX

HURRY UP AND SLOW DOWN!

You slept through the alarm. "Hurry up, or you'll be late for school!" your dad calls. Or you're a competitive swimmer. If you train hard, you know you could trim a few seconds off the time it takes you to do the backstroke in a 25-meter pool. Some occasions call for speeding up.

Others call for slowing down. You and your best friend are enjoying a leisurely paddle in your canoe—and you find yourself wishing the afternoon would never end. Or you're at the top of Toronto's CN Tower and you take a deep breath as you enjoy the view. The last thing you want to do is check the time—or hurry home (unless you have a fear of heights!).

It's useful to know when to hurry and when to slow down. And here's another question worth considering: how can we use our time in a way that brings us happiness?

"Time you enjoy wasting is not wasted time."

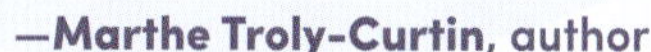

—Marthe Troly-Curtin, author

On Your Mark, Get Set, Go

First Men's 100-Meter Record | Stockholm, Sweden |  1912

In 1912 Donald Lippincott, from the United States, set the first world record in the men's 100-meter sprint at the Stockholm Olympics. At the time we are writing this book, the fastest man in the world is Usain Bolt, a Jamaican sprinter and Olympic gold medalist. In 2009 he set the world record in the 100-meter sprint, completing it in 9.58 seconds at the IAAF World Championships in Athletics. But even if we're not Olympic contenders, speed *can* matter to us. Wouldn't you rather get your homework done in an hour than have it take three hours?

The Downside of Speed

Cognitive scientists have coined the term ***speed-accuracy trade-off*** to explain that there can be a downside to speed. Faster is not always better. When we rush we are more likely to make mistakes. Many car accidents are caused by drivers who exceed the speed limit. In 2021, according to the US Department of Transportation, 29 percent of all traffic deaths were connected to speeding.

PETER DAZELEY/GETTY IMAGES

Life Without a Clock

Puvirnituq, Nunavik — 1960s

Rosie Ivillaq was born in 1960 at her family's hunting camp outside Puvirnituq in Nunavik. When she was growing up, Rosie, who is Inuit, gave little thought to time. "We never focused on time. Everything felt the same. Our ancestors didn't even have a clock. They followed the light and the darkness," Rosie says. Time started to matter more when Rosie was eight and her family moved to town so she could attend school. "I needed to remember school hours," she recalls. Today Rosie is a special education teacher in Puvirnituq. "Now time controls us," she says. "I have to be at school for 8:45 and make supper at 6:30. It was better before."

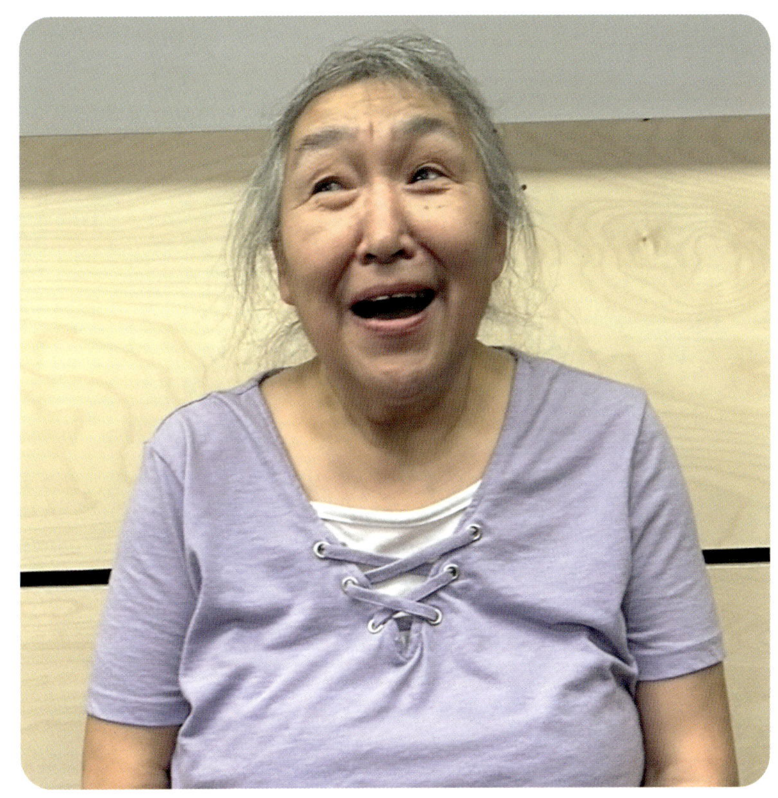

Rosie Ivillaq and her husband both work at Iguarsivik School in Puvirnituq. Located on the Hudson Bay coast, the village of Puvirnituq can only be accessed by airplane.

(TOP) MONIQUE POLAK; (BOTTOM) MARTB/GETTY IMAGES

Overwork Can Be Deadly

First Recorded Case of Karoshi | Tokyo, Japan |  1969

Karoshi is the Japanese word for death from vascular diseases (such as heart attacks and strokes), mental disorders or suicide, caused by overwork. The term was coined in the 1970s, after the first recorded case of karoshi. Today the term is used around the world. Overwork, or spending more time working than is good for you, has become an international problem. A study by the World Health Organization (WHO) found that, in 2016, working long hours led to the deaths of more than 745,000 people. The WHO concluded that "working 55 hours or more per week is a serious health hazard."

The Japanese government has made efforts to put an end to karoshi. In 1987 the government changed the country's labor standards law, making 40 the maximum number of hours an individual could be required to work in a week. This is more in line with laws in other countries. The following year, the Japanese government—together with the country's doctors—set up a karoshi hotline enabling overworked citizens to get support and advice.

"Since time is the one immaterial object which we cannot influence—neither speed up nor slow down, add to nor diminish—it is an imponderably valuable gift."

—**Maya Angelou**, author

Spending Wisely

There's an old expression that says *Time is money*. But how we *spend* our time is up to each of us—and that decision helps to make us who we are. Are you the kind of kid who can focus all day Sunday on doing homework—or do you prioritize hanging out with friends and family? Maybe you'd like to find a balance between work and leisure?

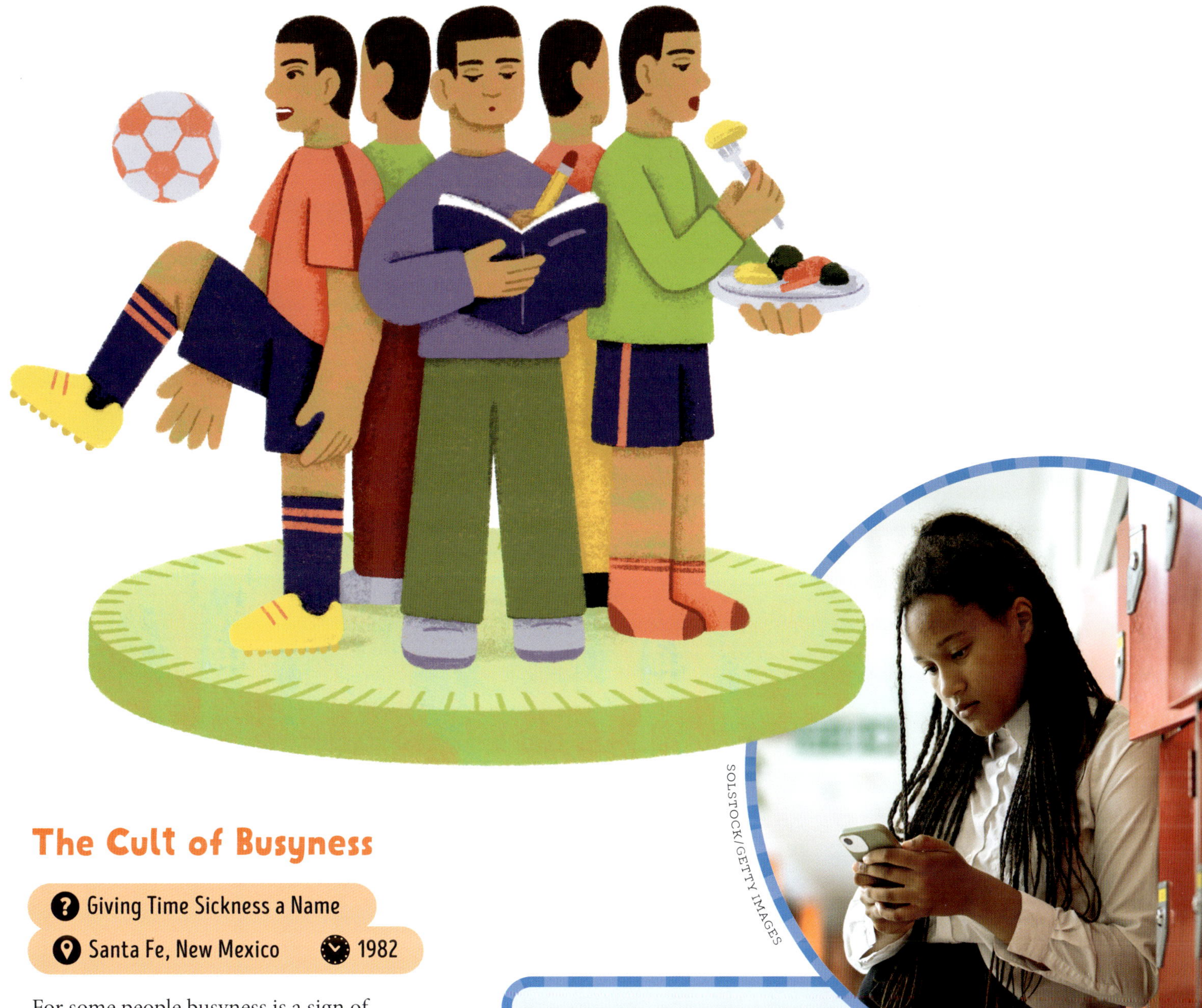

SOLSTOCK/GETTY IMAGES

The Cult of Busyness

Giving Time Sickness a Name

Santa Fe, New Mexico 1982

For some people busyness is a sign of success. Being busy can make us feel important. Consider the Hollywood actor who must turn down a film role because she is already acting in two films that are expected to be blockbusters!

But chronic busyness—which means rarely having time to take a break—can lead to fatigue and stress. In 1982 American author and physician Larry Dossey coined the term ***time sickness*** to describe the feeling that we are running out of time and must speed up to keep up.

FOMO

FOMO is an acronym for "fear of missing out." The term was first used in 2004 and made it into the *Oxford Dictionary* in 2013. FOMO helps explain why some people have trouble saying no, which can lead them to take on too much, which in turn can lead to their feeling they are too busy and that they have too little time. Regular exposure to social networking sites like Instagram and TikTok contributes to FOMO. When we are bombarded by images and descriptions of what everyone else is doing with their time, it's no wonder we feel as though we are missing out.

Playing chess is not only fun but also helps develop problem-solving skills.
AZMANL/GETTY IMAGES

Another Perspective Altogether

Kinship Time | **Past, Present and Future**

Kyle Powys Whyte is known for his research on climate change and its effect on Indigenous Peoples.
KYLE WHYTE/WIKIMEDIA COMMONS/ CC BY-SA 4.0

For most people in the western world, time is linear and future-oriented. Indigenous Peoples—those who inhabited the land before colonists arrived—tend to see time as cyclical and closely connected to the seasons.

Kyle Powys Whyte, who teaches at the University of Michigan School for Environment and Sustainability, is a member of the Citizen Potawatomi Nation. Whyte has written about ***kinship time***. Instead of focusing on productivity and getting things done as quickly as possible, kinship time focuses on forming relationships and coming up with solutions without a deadline.

To demonstrate what he means by kinship time, Whyte compares a timed chess game to one in which there is no ticking clock. "I can imagine," Whyte writes, "a chess game where I can consult others widely, take my long-term health seriously and balance the game workload with caretaking duties to my family and society."

Slow Down, You Move Too Fast!

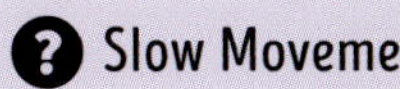 Slow Movement · London, England ·  1986

When he caught himself rushing through a bedtime story he was reading to his son, journalist Carl Honoré realized he needed to slow down. Honoré, who went on to write *In Praise of Slow: How a Worldwide Movement Is Challenging the Cult of Speed,* is a leader in the global slow movement.

Like others in the movement, which started in 1986 with protests against fast food, Honoré urges us to "savor the hours and minutes rather than just counting them." Although he appreciates speed, he reminds us that we need to do our best—which often requires slowing down and paying attention. "It's about quality over quantity in everything from work to food to parenting," he writes.

To ***accelerate*** is to begin to move more quickly. When drivers put a foot on the accelerator, they pick up speed. The more we cram into our days, the more texts we send and read, and the more video games we play, the more we feel as if we are accelerating. To ***decelerate*** is the opposite. It's an attempt to move more slowly.

Take Your Foot Off the Gas

Deceleration is an important part of athletic training. It's better not to jump off a stationary bicycle when you've been going full speed. It's safer to take the time for a few minutes of cool-down cycling. Deceleration helps increase agility and prevent injury. Deceleration isn't only for athletes. Other deceleration activities we can all practice include going for a walk (especially in nature), sitting on a park bench, petting our dogs, listening to music, doing yoga and meditating.

KLAUS VEDFELT/GETTY IMAGES

TOPDESIGNER/GETTY IMAGES

An Endless Loop

Groundhog Day Movie | Punxsutawney, Pennsylvania |  1993

In the 1993 movie *Groundhog Day*, a weatherman named Phil Connors (played by actor Bill Murray) is forced to relive the same day over and over again. Connors is trapped in an endless loop. The comedy made viewers laugh, but many also found it frustrating to watch.

Connors was obviously wasting his time! Or was he? Because thanks to all that repetition, Connors learned a thing or two. He used the knowledge he gained to save lives, find and appreciate true love, and learn new skills such as playing the piano and ice sculpting.

Punxsutawney residents claim that their groundhog, Punxsutawney Phil, has been making predictions since 1886 and that he owes his long life to a mysterious beverage called "the elixir of life."

ANTHONY QUINTANO/WIKIMEDIA COMMONS/CC BY-SA 2.0

Siesta Snooze

Compulsory Siesta Law  Ador, Spain 2015

In Spanish the word ***siesta*** means an afternoon nap. The word is derived from the Latin *sexta*, or sixth hour. Because, as far back as the second century, the Romans counted their hours from sunrise, the sixth hour of their day fell in the afternoon. That was when Romans paused to eat and rest.

Siesta is common in Mediterranean countries, southern Europe and Latin America as well as in parts of China and India. Siesta often takes place at the hottest time of day, making it a well-deserved break for those working outdoors.

Though the word *siesta* comes to us from Spanish, most Spaniards do not take siestas. According to the BBC, some 60 percent of Spaniards never have a siesta. That may be why Joan Faus Vitòria, mayor of Ador, a Spanish town near Valencia, passed a law in 2015 making a daily siesta between two and five in the afternoon compulsory in summertime. The law also applies to kids—parents are supposed to keep them indoors during siesta time.

Siestapp

A ***somnologist*** studies sleep. According to Spanish somnologist Juan José Ortega-Albás, "a brief siesta helps us to alleviate stress, strengthens the immune system and improves performance." How brief is brief? Some somnologists recommend we get between 20 and 30 minutes of rest in order to derive the benefits of a daytime nap. Software developers approve of napping too. They've developed sleep optimization apps—such as Siestapp—to help us get those daytime z's.

Pandemic Pace

COVID-19 Pandemic 2020

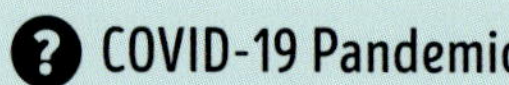

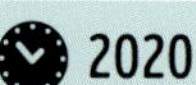

"Lost time is never found again."
—Benjamin Franklin, Founding Father of the United States

On March 11, 2020, the WHO declared COVID-19 a pandemic. Because so many businesses and schools around the world shut down, and there were fewer opportunities to socialize, life slowed down for many of us. Some people—and this includes kids—enjoyed the break from routine initially. Until boredom set in. But one surprising result of the pandemic was the people who reported enjoying the slower pace! Even when the pandemic was over and it was safe to return to work and school and see our friends, these people decided they'd prefer to spend their time differently, living with a shorter to-do list, rushing around less and being less busy.

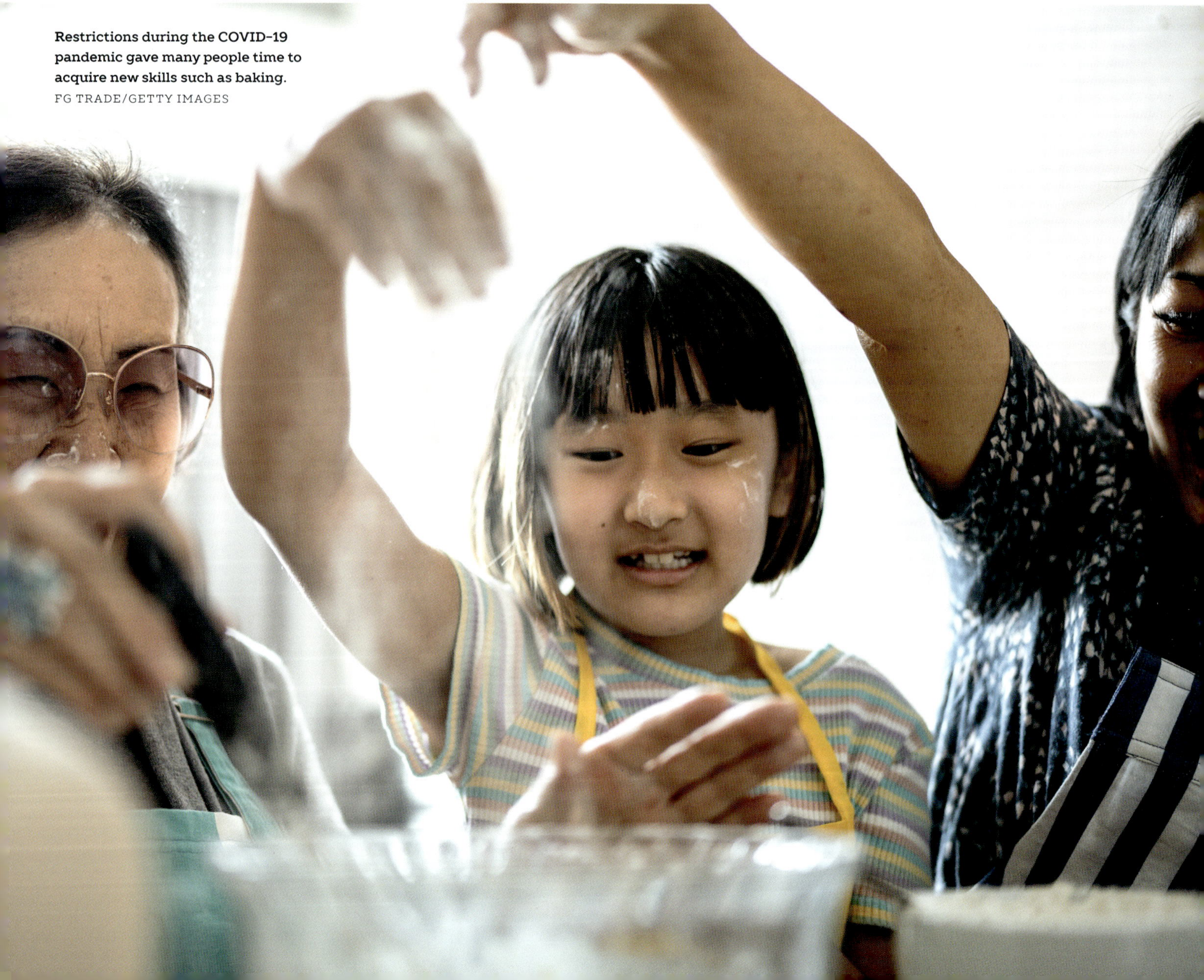

Restrictions during the COVID-19 pandemic gave many people time to acquire new skills such as baking.
FG TRADE/GETTY IMAGES

Living in the Moment

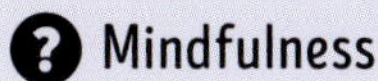
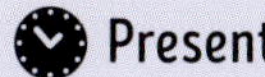

Mindfulness Present

Have you ever heard the expression *The present is a present*? It's easy to get caught up thinking about the past ("If only I had studied for that test") or planning for the future ("What can I do to make next weekend special?"). Of course, learning from the past and planning for the future are useful activities. But there are tricks for staying in—and appreciating—the present.

Mindfulness is a cognitive skill that can be developed. Here are four ways to help you become more mindful.

1. **Breathe deeply.** Taking deep belly breaths calms the nervous system and helps you focus on the moment.

2. **Savor.** As the expression goes, *Stop and smell the roses.* Even better, make an effort to use all five of your senses. Really look at those roses. Listen to the breeze; feel it on your cheeks. Taste that salted-caramel ice cream.

3. **Keep a journal.** Even if you write only a paragraph a day (or even once a week), journaling is another way to focus on the moment.

4. **Color.** Choosing colors and then coloring a picture turns out to be another great way to reduce stress and cultivate mindfulness.

AAMORIM/GETTY IMAGES

JORDI SALAS/GETTY IMAGES

WESTEND61/GETTY IMAGES

POLLYANA VENTURA/GETTY IMAGES

1947
Launch of
Doomsday clock
FUTURE
The Seedling
Project
3797
1555
Nostradamus
predicts end
of the world
2500 BCE
First plastic
surgeries

SEVEN

RUNNING OUT OF TIME

There is no stopping time. All things come to an end. That includes lazy Sunday afternoons, summer holidays, books and, of course, us too. No matter our age, we are all passing through time. It's hard to imagine your newborn cousin will one day be a teenager and eventually a senior citizen. Or that the elderly gentleman who lives down the hall from you was ever a baby!

It's only human to be concerned with getting older and eventually dying. Mortality is a consequence of time. But it can help to take a lesson from geologists, who study the vastness of time. If we are each just a speck in time, perhaps we can live in a way that might help improve the lives of those who will come after us.

1875–1997
Jeanne Louise Calment lives to 122 years old

An Attempt to Stop Time

First Plastic Surgeries | Ancient Egypt | 2500 BCE

The earliest ***plastic surgeries*** date to around 2500 BCE, when they were performed for reconstruction after injuries like a broken nose. Reconstructive cosmetic surgeries remain common.

But nowadays more and more people are turning to purely cosmetic surgeries and procedures as a way to fight off some of the physical signs of aging like wrinkles and saggy skin.

Not Everyone Likes Getting Old

You might like the idea of getting older. Not only will you be tall enough to reach stuff you couldn't reach before, but you will have more independence when you are grown up. Many adults, however, fear the aging process. This fear is so common it has a name: ***gerascophobia***.

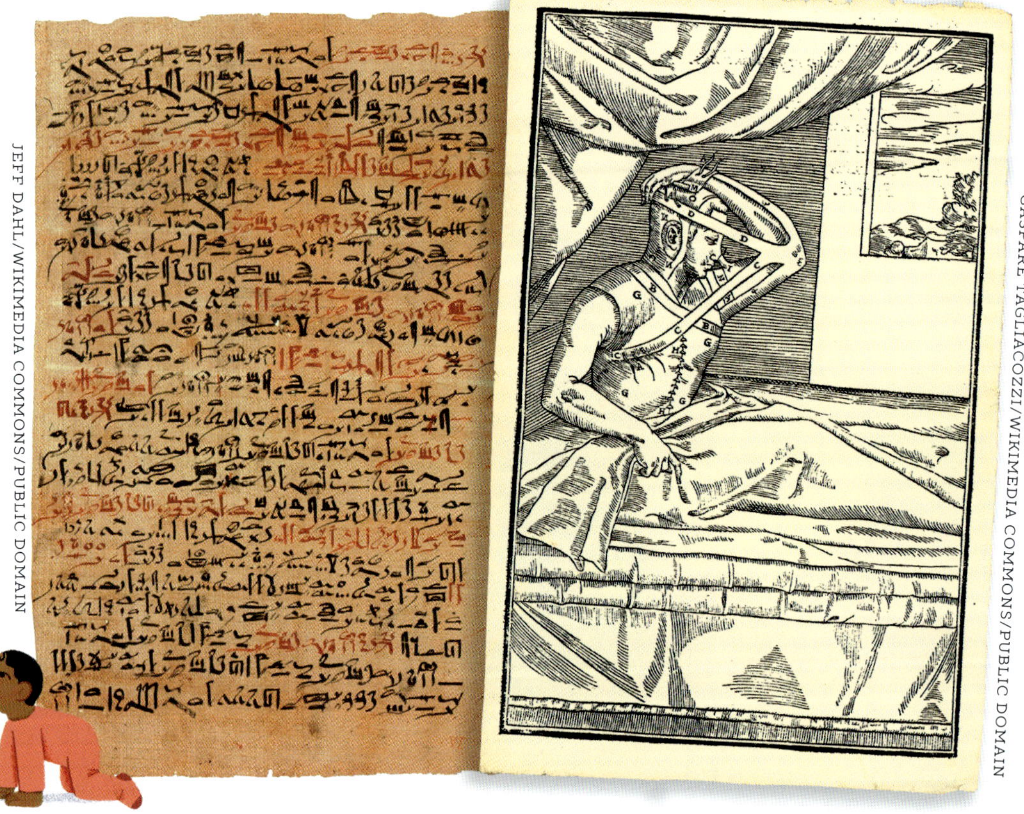

JEFF DAHL/WIKIMEDIA COMMONS/PUBLIC DOMAIN

GASPARE TAGLIACOZZI/WIKIMEDIA COMMONS/PUBLIC DOMAIN

The Edwin Smith Papyrus, an ancient Egyptian text named after the antique dealer who purchased it in 1862, is believed to contain the first mention of plastic surgery.

Super-Aging!

People might be less afraid of aging if they knew they would one day be ***super-agers***, a term that refers to individuals who are 80 or older and whose brains age at a slower rate than average. Jeanne Louise Calment is believed to be the oldest person who ever lived. Born in 1875 in Arles, France, she lived until 1997, shortly after celebrating her 122nd birthday. ***Longevity*** experts deemed Calment a super-ager. Although she did try smoking as a young woman, she only took up smoking regularly at the age of 112. Calment had the following sensible advice for younger people: "If you can't do anything about it, don't worry."

WIKIMEDIA COMMONS/PUBLIC DOMAIN

The astrological clock at the Cathedral of Our Lady of Chartres, France.
(MAIN) B. VAN/SHUTTERSTOCK.COM; (INSET) GWENGOAT/GETTY IMAGES

Long History of Wondering

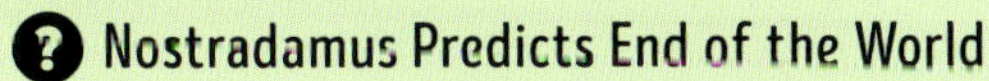
Nostradamus Predicts End of the World

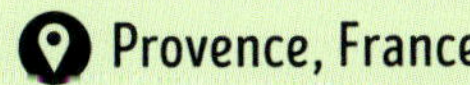
Provence, France

1555

Even mountains come to an end, thanks to erosion. It's natural for us to wonder about the end of time. Will the world as we know it come to an end one day? And if so, then what?

There's nothing new about wondering—and worrying—about the end of time. Back in the 16th century, French astrologer Nostradamus predicted the world would end in the year 3797. Nostradamus published his prophecies in 1555 in a book called *Centuries*. The book contained 942 predictions, each one expressed in a rhyming quatrain, or four-line verse. Many people consider Nostradamus to have been a fake. Others credit him for having predicted the rise of Napoleon and Hitler, and even the COVID-19 pandemic. One thing we know for sure is that Nostradamus's writing style is extremely vague, making it easier for those who claim his predictions were accurate.

Counting Down

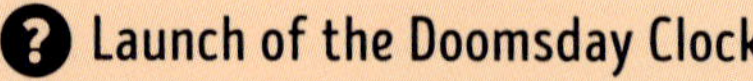 Launch of the Doomsday Clock · Chicago, Illinois ·  1947

Doomsday is a term used to refer to the end of the world. Just the word itself sounds depressing. Maybe it's the double *d*'s. Or that the word *doom* means a horrible fate.

Nuclear war is one of the greatest threats to our world. Atomic bombs dropped over the Japanese cities of Hiroshima and Nagasaki in 1945 brought an end to World War II, but had devastating consequences—killing and injuring thousands of civilians, and later leading to some 60,000 deaths due to exposure to radiation.

Between 1946 and 1958, after the attacks on Hiroshima and Nagasaki, the United States detonated nuclear weapons on Bikini Atoll in the Marshall Islands.
ARCHIVE HOLDINGS INC./GETTY IMAGES

A ***nuclear arms race***—the accumulation of nuclear weapons by different countries—between the United States and what was then the Soviet Union began in the 1940s. Since then other countries, including Iran, China, India, Israel and North Korea, have joined the nuclear arms race. That has many people worried.

In 1947 members of the Bulletin of the Atomic Scientists, a nonprofit media organization, launched the ***Doomsday Clock***. It was set at seven minutes to midnight as a concrete reminder of how close the world was then to nuclear destruction—midnight being the point when that destruction would come.

Since then the hands on the Doomsday Clock have been moved more than 20 times. In 1991, after then–US president George H.W. Bush met with Soviet leader Mikhail Gorbachev and announced a reduction in their countries' arms arsenals, the time on the Doomsday Clock was reset to 17 minutes before midnight. More recently, in January 2025, in response to factors including the war in Ukraine, the conflict in the Middle East, the threat of nuclear war and the impact of climate change, the Bulletin of Atomic Scientists moved the hands of the Doomsday Clock forward to just 89 seconds before midnight.

The Doomsday Clock continues to remind us of the ongoing threats to our planet, whether from climate change, nuclear weapons or political upheaval. Its purpose is not only to warn us about these threats but also to inspire us to stand up and take action.

The Doomsday Clock has never reached midnight—which would mark the end of humanity.
PUTTAPON/GETTY IMAGES, RYANICUS GIRRAFICUS/WIKIMEDIA COMMONS/CC0

A Chilling Attempt to Overcome Death

First Cryogenic Freezing | Glendale, California |  1967

It's pretty chilly at -202°F (-130°C). That is the temperature required for a process known as ***cryogenic freezing***—a method to preserve dead bodies with the hope of one day being able to restore them to life. In 1967 American psychology professor James Bedford became the first person ever to be cryogenically frozen following his death. The procedure, which today costs about US $30,000, involves draining bodily fluids, replacing them with special chemicals, then storing the body in a deep freeze. Most scientists agree that cryonics is a scam. They point out that no one has ever been revived and that the cryogenics industry profits by giving people false hope.

In the movie *The Empire Strikes Back*, the fictional character Han Solo is frozen in carbonite. This model is on display at a shopping center in Bangkok, Thailand.
SARUNYU L/SHUTTERSTOCK.COM

Hollywood Portrays the End of Time

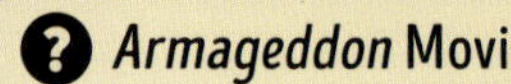
Armageddon Movie

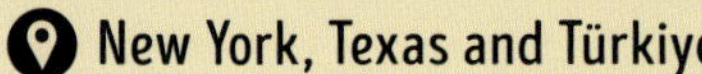
New York, Texas and Türkiye

1998

Good versus Evil

The word ***Armageddon*** refers to the place where a battle is fought between good and evil. The term is found in the Bible's New Testament.

Armageddon, released in 1998, was a popular sci-fi disaster movie. In it, a group of oil drillers hired by NASA have 18 days to stop an asteroid from striking Earth. The animated sci-fi movie *WALL-E*, released in 2008, is set in 2805 and tells the story of a robot sent to clean up an uninhabited Earth. Even ***zombie movies***, such as the 2018 musical horror movie *Zombies*, deal with the end of time. In this popular genre, zombies are corpses who have come back to life—meaning they've already reached the end of their time on Earth as humans.

In 2013 a meteor almost the size of a tennis court entered Earth's atmosphere over Chelyabinsk, Russia.
SOLARSEVEN/GETTY IMAGES

World Survives the Year 2000

? Y2K | New Zealand | 2000

Back in the mid-'90s people started worrying about the approach of Y2K—the year 2000. Computer experts were the first to sound the alarm. They were concerned that unless the tech world was well-prepared, computers might not be able to deal with the year 2000. That's because software engineers had always represented the year using two digits. They feared that the move at precisely midnight of January 1 from 99 (the last two digits of 1999) to 00 (the last two digits of 2000) might wipe out not only computers but also cell phones, cars, trains and airplanes—and much more. The US government spent some $70 billion preparing for a possible Y2K calamity. Y2K disaster kits—complete with ***abacus***, flashlight and compass—became a hot commodity.

The rest of the world watched anxiously when the clock struck midnight in New Zealand, which is 18 hours ahead of those living in the Eastern Standard Time zone. We heaved a giant collective sigh of relief when New Zealand's computers, cars, trains and airplanes made it into the new century without a blip!

Y2K **means "year 2000." The** ***Y*** **stands for "year" and the** ***K*** **stands for "kilo," used to refer to a unit of 1,000.**
ABLESTOCK/GETTY IMAGES

Thinking Ahead

The Long Time Project

London, England  **2018**

British activists Ella Saltmarshe and Beatrice Pembroke believe solutions to big problems require looking far, far ahead. That's why, in 2018, the pair founded the Long Time Project. Saltmarshe and Pembroke urge us—as well as policymakers and artists of all kinds—to think more about the generations that will succeed us. Their guide reminds us that "long time behavior seeks to cultivate an attitude of care for the future...so that we change our behavior in the present."

> "All we have to decide is what to do with the time that is given us."
>
> —J.R.R. Tolkien, author

Long-Term Thinking

Timefulness

Appleton, Wisconsin  **2018**

Geologist Marcia Bjornerud, a professor at Wisconsin's Lawrence University, is credited for coming up with the word ***timefulness***. In 2018 she published a book with that title, subtitled *How Thinking Like a Geologist Can Help Save the World*. For Bjornerud, timefulness means thinking in the long, long term—as in hundreds of years into the future. Bjornerud believes we have become "time illiterate," too focused on the short term. She urges ordinary citizens as well as policymakers to think beyond ourselves and our own time, and to consider our effect on nature. Yet even with all the problems humanity and our planet are facing, Bjornerud remains optimistic. She told an interviewer she takes comfort "in knowing that I am a resident of an ancient, resilient, marvelously complicated planet that has been teeming with life and continuously reinventing itself for four billion years."

The Climate Crisis

- Heat Dome
- British Columbia, Canada
- 2021

Planet Earth is heating up. Since 1880 the Earth's average temperature has increased by 1.9°F (1.1°C). Global warming has been shown to lead to more extreme weather events such as ice storms, hurricanes, tsunamis and wildfires. Here's just one example: in the summer of 2021, 619 people in British Columbia died from heat-related causes when a heat dome raised temperatures 20 degrees above seasonal norms—proof that humans and other animals are finding it hard to adapt to rising temperatures.

You Can Help!

Experts agree that by making small changes in our own lives, every person can help to combat global warming and protect our planet for future generations. Here are some simple ways kids can help.

Walk or bike (or use public transit) whenever possible instead of getting a car ride from your parents.

Turn off the lights when you leave a room.

Shut down your computer when you have finished using it.

Ask your parents to reduce the temperature in your home—68°F (20°C) is warm enough. If it isn't, put on a sweater!

Take shorter showers.

Recycle.

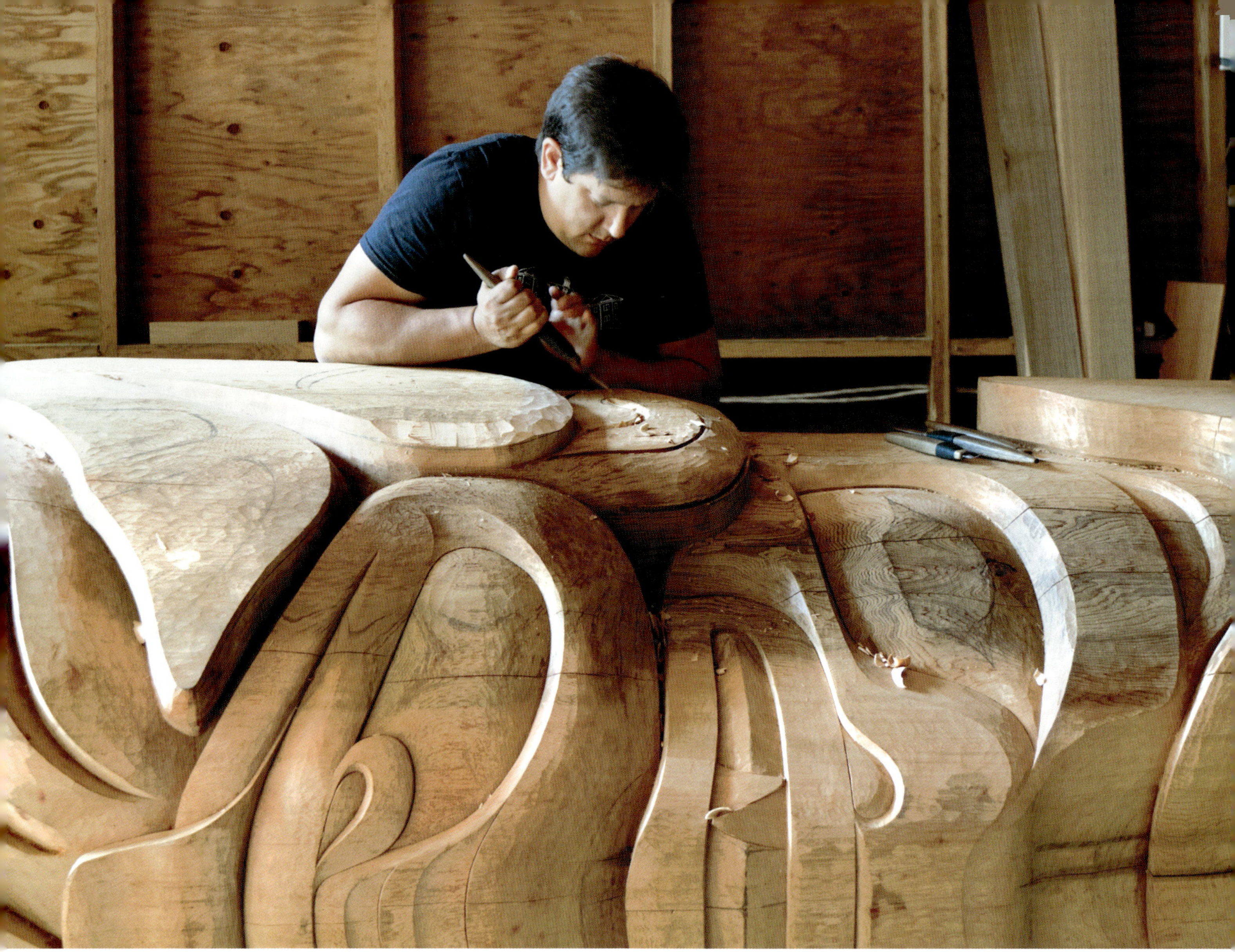

Some of Carey Newman's totems are carved out of old-growth cedar, but today he's also carving with second-growth trees. He says he made that decision because he feels a sense of responsibility to protect the old-growth trees that are left.
ANDREW QUERNER

Slow Art

The Seedling Project | Victoria, British Columbia | Future

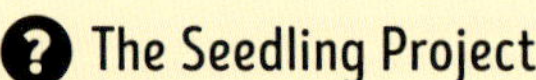

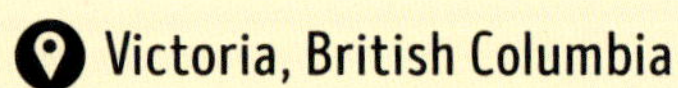

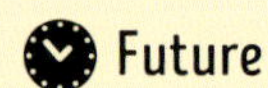

Carey Newman is a Kwakwa̱ka̱'wakw artist and master carver in Victoria, British Columbia. He plans to plant a western red cedar on the grounds of the University of Victoria that will be carved into a totem pole by artists hundreds of years in the future, when the tree is fully grown. Newman will design the pole using 3D technology and store it for the future. He says the Seedling Project means thinking about radically different timelines for art and coming up with plans for how the tree will be cared for and protected on the university grounds in the centuries *before* it's carved. "When it comes to addressing big issues like climate change or deforestation, our solutions need to span many generations," says Newman. "To achieve this we need to make plans and agreements that live longer than the people who make them."

Borrowed Time

Call to Action All of Us  Future

The expression *borrowed time* refers to living with an uncertain period of time that will end with something unavoidable, such as—well—death. Some people might find this a depressing end to our book—but for us, it isn't. The fact that our time is limited is a kind of call to action—and to life itself. None of us knows how much time we will have on Earth, but that knowledge (or lack of knowledge) is a reminder to enjoy whatever time we have—in whatever ways feel right to us. Perhaps that includes devoting some of our time to meaningful projects, such as making our world a little better for those who will come after us.

"Yesterday is gone. Tomorrow has not yet come. We only have today. Let us begin."

—Mother Teresa, Catholic nun and saint

Tree planting helps protect the earth. Trees filter the air, reduce soil erosion, regulate water cycles and provide habitat for wildlife.
HALFPOINT IMAGES/GETTY IMAGES

UNDEFINED UNDEFINED/GETTY IMAGES

GLOSSARY

abacus—a hand-operated instrument for counting

accelerate—to begin to move more quickly

Armageddon—the place where a battle is fought between good and evil

atomic clock—a highly accurate timekeeping device that measures time by monitoring the resonant frequency of cesium atoms

chronoculture—a way of growing crops that works with plants' circadian rhythms

circadian rhythms—natural changes occurring over a 24-hour cycle

cryogenic freezing—a method of preserving dead bodies with the hope of one day in the future being able to restore them to life, considered a scam by most scientists

daylight saving time—a strategy to optimize daylight in which the clock jumps ahead by an hour in March and falls back an hour in November

decelerate—an attempt to move more slowly

deep time—occurs when we lose track of time, especially when we are doing something we enjoy

digital clock—a timekeeping device that displays the time in numerical digits

doomsday—the day on which some horrible fate will occur

Doomsday Clock—a design launched in 1947 by members of the Bulletin of the Atomic Scientists to remind us how close the world is to nuclear destruction

electric clock—a timekeeping device powered by a high-voltage battery; an electric impulse operates the clock's dials

fossil record—the history of life on Earth as indicated by fossils

gerascophobia—an excessive fear of aging

GPS—an acronym for global positioning system, a satellite-based radio navigating system

grandfather clock—a clock enclosed in a tall wooden case and powered by a pendulum

Greenwich Mean Time (GMT)—the single standard time counted from midnight at the Royal Observatory in Greenwich, England, based on the yearly average (mean) of the time each day when the sun crosses the prime meridian at Greenwich. When the sun is at its highest point, exactly above the prime meridian, it's noon at Greenwich.

hippocampus—the part of the brain connected to memory and learning

hourglass—a timekeeping device consisting of two clear glass globes attached by a narrow neck that allows sand to flow from the upper to the lower globe; can be used to measure an hour or a minute

hypothalamus—the area of the brain that produces hormones controlling functions such as body temperature, hunger and mood

karoshi—a Japanese word for death caused by overwork

kinship time—a way of using time that focuses on forming relationships and coming up with solutions without a deadline

longevity—the long duration of an individual life

mechanical clock—a timekeeping device with moving parts, including a descending weight and gear wheels

mechanical watch—a timekeeping device with a mainspring that can be wound up

migrations—movements from one place to another

mindfulness—awareness of your body and mind in the present

mythology—a collection of stories from a certain culture, or the study of those stories

neurons—cells that receive and send messages

nuclear arms race—the accumulation of nuclear weapons by different countries

nuclear war—a war in which atomic weapons are used

opportunistic time—a term for when the time is right

pendulum—a hanging weight that swings backward and forward

plastic surgeries—surgeries to reconstruct or alter the human body

popular culture—the cultural information we absorb from popular sources like comics, movies and TV

quartz clock—a timekeeping devices that uses quartz crystals. They are inexpensive and quite accurate.

resonant frequency—the natural frequency at which an object vibrates

shadow clock (or sun stick)—a timekeeping device invented by ancient Egyptians and Babylonians who noted the changes in the shadow cast by the stick

shift work—a work schedule that's outside the usual nine-to-five

siesta—a Spanish word for afternoon nap

somnologist—someone who studies sleep

speed-accuracy trade-off—a term for the downside of rushing, which is that when we rush, we are more likely to make mistakes

striatum—a part of the basal ganglia in the brain that is involved in decision-making functions such as motor control and emotion

sundial—a timekeeping device that measures time by the length or direction of the shadow cast by a gnomon

super-ager—a term used for people aged 80 or older whose brains age at a slower rate than average

suprachiasmatic nucleus (SCN)—the master timekeeper of circadian rhythms in the brain

theologian—someone who studies religion

time blindness—the phenomenon in which people lose awareness of the passage of time

time sickness—a term for the feeling that we are running out of time and must speed up to keep up

timefulness—a term coined by geologist Marcia Bjornerud that refers to thinking in the long, long term, as in hundreds of years into the future

water clock—a timekeeping device consisting of a bowl filled with water that dripped out at a steady rate. Lines inscribed inside the bowl indicated each passing hour.

zeptosecond—the shortest unit of time ever measured

zombie movies—a popular movie genre in which corpses come back to life and return to Earth

Zoroastrianism—a religion originating in ancient Persia (now called Iran) that is believed to be one of the world's oldest religions still in existence

RESOURCES

Print

Carroll, Lewis. *Alice's Adventures in Wonderland.* Macmillan, 1865.

Ferrón, Sheddad Kaid-Salah. *My First Book of Relativity.* Button Book, 2019.

L'Engle, Madeleine. *A Wrinkle in Time.* Farrar, Straus and Giroux, 1962.

Maestro, Betsy. *The Story of Clocks and Calendars.* HarperCollins, 2004.

A Street Through Time: A 12,000-Year Journey Along the Same Street. DK Children, 2020.

Timelines of Everything: From Woolly Mammoths to World Wars. DK Children, 2018.

Tyson, Neil deGrasse, with Gregory Mone. *Astrophysics for Young People in a Hurry.* W.W. Norton, 2019.

Online

American Clock & Watch Museum: clockandwatchmuseum.org

Biological Clock: kids.britannica.com/students/article/biological-clock/273219

Canadian Clock Museum: canclockmuseum.ca

Clocks and Timekeeping: kids.britannica.com/students/article/clock/605080

Dogs Can Tell Time: discovermagazine.com/planet-earth/how-dogs-perceive-time

Doomsday Clock: thebulletin.org/doomsday-clock

Greenwich Mean Time: rmg.co.uk/stories/topics/greenwich-mean-time-gmt

History of Time: astronomy.com/science/a-brief-history-of-time-what-is-it-and-how-do-we-define-it

Lunar Time: newsforkids.net/articles/2023/03/02/how-do-you-tell-time-on-the-moon

Make Your Own Sundial: pbs.org/parents/crafts-and-experiments/diy-sundial

Monarch Butterfly Migration: monarchjointventure.org

Museum of Timekeeping: museumoftimekeeping.org.uk

Phases of the Moon: spaceplace.nasa.gov/moon-phases/en

ACKNOWLEDGMENTS

A big thank-you to Monique Polak. Even though we live several time zones apart, when we both said we wanted to write about time, it was an easy decision to say, "Let's do it together!" Thanks also to Dana L. Church for her expertise and keen eye. And, of course, it takes a pod to make a book, so thanks go to everyone at Orca Book Publishers, including Georgia Bradburne, Ruth Linka, Vivian Sinclair and Dahlia Yuen, and illustrator Paige Stampatori. Thanks to my family for giving me the time to write in all the fun busyness of our life together. —K.H.

Special thanks to Kirstie Hudson. This was my first time having a coauthor—and I could not have picked one who was smarter, kinder or more fun. Thanks also to my friends in Puvirnituq, Nunavik—especially to Rosie Ivillaq, who turned up at just the right time and shared what it was like to grow up without a clock. Thanks to the entire Orca pod for bringing our book to life, and to Paige Stampatori for her illustrations. Thanks to my husband, Guy Rouleau, for his timely suggestions and careful reading of our manuscript. My happiest moments in time are spent with you. —M.P.

INDEX

*Page numbers in **bold** indicate an image caption.*

abacus, 75, 81
aging
 gerascophobia, 70, 81
 oldest person, **69**, 70
 perception of time, 44–45
 reversal of, **37**, 45
agriculture
 chronoculture, **46**, 54–**55**, 81
 vertical farms, 54–**55**
Alice's Adventures in Wonderland (Carroll), **4**, 10, 30
analog clock display, 32, 33
Androsthenes, 48
animals, internal clocks, 47, 48, 49–51
archaeological record, 16–17, 26
Armageddon (movie), 74
Armageddon, defined, 74, 81
astrological clock, **71**
atomic clocks, **14**, 21, 22, 34, 81
Augustine of Hippo, Saint, **36**, 38

Babylonians, ancient, 17, 19, 26, 27
Back to the Future (movie), **4**, 12
Bejan, Adrian, 44
birds, 48
Bjornerud, Marcia, 76
brain research
 and sleep, 39–41, 43, 65
 time cells, 42–43, 50–51

calendars, 16–17
Calment, Jeanne Louise, **69**, 70
children
 circadian rhythms, 40
 learning to tell time, 32
China, ancient, 16, 27
chronoculture, **46**, 54–**55**, 81
Chronos, Aiôn and Kaïros, **4**, 6
circadian rhythms
 defined, 39, 81
 plants and animals, 47–55
 research, **36**, 39–41, 43
 See also internal clocks; natural cycles
Clement, William, 29
climate crisis, 2, 53, 77
clockmakers, 29–33
clock time. *See* measurement of time
clockwise, origin of, 27
communication, 22, 34
Coordinated Lunar Time, **14**, 23
Coordinated Universal Time (UTC), 21
COVID-19 pandemic, 66
cryogenic freezing, 73, 81
Curious Case of Benjamin Button, The, 13

daylight saving time (DST), 2, 35, 81
deep time, 6, 81
de Mairan, Jean-Jacques d'Ortous, 48
digital clock display, **24**, 25, 32, 33, 34, 81
Dinosaur Provincial Park, AB, **52**
doomsday
 defined, 72, 81
 in popular culture, 74
Doomsday Clock, **68**, 72, 81

Ecclesiazusae, The (Aristophanes), 19
Egyptians, ancient, 17, 19, 26, 70
electric clocks, 31, 81
Empire Strikes Back, The (movie), 73
employment
 shift work, 40
 and siestas, 65
 work/life balance, 60
Expo 1970 time capsules, 35

Father Time, **4**, 9
"fear of missing out" (FOMO), 61
food production, 54–**55**
fossil record, 16–17, 26, 81
Fox, Michael J., 12
future, long-term planning, 69, 76–79

geologic time, 53, 76
gerascophobia, 70, 81
GPS (global positioning system), 22, 34, 81
grandfather clocks, 29, 81
Greeks, ancient, 6, 19
Greenwich Mean Time (GMT), **14**, 20, 81
Groundhog Day, **64**
Groundhog Day (movie), 64

Hall, Jeffrey C., 41
Hattori, Kintaro, 33
Henlein, Peter, 29
Hinduism, 7
hippocampus, 42, 81
Honoré, Carl, 63
hourglass, 6, **24**, 28, 81

Hudson, George Vernon, 35
human health
 and aging, 44–45
 and jet lag, 43
 monitoring, **33**
 and shift work, 40
 and sleep, 39–41, 43, 65

and stress, 33, 60–61, 65, 67
See also mindfulness
hypothalamus, 41, 81

Indigenous Peoples, 59, 62, 78
insects, 39, 49, 55
internal clocks
of animals, 47, 48, 49–51
brain research, 42–43, 50–51
circadian rhythms, 39–41, 43, 81
plants, 47, 48, 54–**55**
international standard time
atomic clocks, **14**, 21, 22, 34, 81
daylight saving time, 2, 35, 81
Greenwich Mean Time (GMT), **14**, 20, 81
lunar time zone, **14**, 23
Inuit traditional culture, 59
Ivillaq, Rosie, 59

Japan, 35, 60
jet lag, **36**, 43

Kali, Hindu goddess, 7
karoshi, 60, 81
kinship time, **56**, 62, 81
Kleitman, Nathaniel, 39

linear time, 6, 10, 13, 64
Lippincott, Donald, 58
longevity
aging process, 45, 70
cryogenic freezing, 73, 81
Long Time Project, 76
lunar cycle, 16, 17

Mammoth Cave experiment, 39
mammoth-tusk calendars, **14**, 16
measurement of time
accurate, 2, 22, 34, 35
geologic time, 53, 76
hours and minutes, 17–21
resonator devices, 34
seconds, 17, 22
zeptoseconds, 2, 82
mechanical clocks and watches, 29, 82
mercury (in water clock), 27
migrations, 16, **46**, 49, 82
mindfulness
defined, 67, 82
and nature, 44, 63
tips towards, 64, 67
minutes and seconds
accurate, 22, 34
zeptoseconds, 2, 34
Monarch butterfly migration, **46**, 49
moon (lunar cycle), 16, 17
mythology, 6–9, 82

natural cycles
and circadian rhythms, 39–41, 43, 81
measurement of time, 15–19
and migrations, 16, 49, 82
plants and animals, 47–55
seasons, 6, 15, 48, 62
sunlight and shadows, 17–19, 26
traditional cultures, 59, 62
Newman, Carey, 78
Norse mythology, 8
Nostradamus, **68**, 71
nuclear war, 72, 82

opportunistic time, 6, 82

pace of life
and aging, 44
choice of activity, 63, 65–67
and making mistakes, 43, 58
and stress, 57, 60–63
traditional, 59, 62
Pembroke, Beatrice, 76
pendulum clocks, 29, 34, 82
perception of time
and aging, 44
animals, 50–51
mindfulness, 44, 63, 64, 67, 82
slow movement, 44, **56**, 63
subjective time, 1, 6
time blindness, 33, 82
pets, 47, 50–51
phrenology, **36**, 38
plants, internal clocks, 47, 48, 54–**55**
plastic surgeries, **68**, 70, 82
Plato clock, 32
plutonium clocks, **24**, 35
pocket watches, 30
popular culture
cryogenic freezing, 73, 81
defined, 9, 82
disaster movies, 74
fantasy, 10
and mythology, 8
time loop, 64
time travel, 11–13
predictions
disaster, 74, 75
Doomsday Clock, 72
end of the world, **68**, 71, 72
of Nostradamus, 71
ptarmigans, 48

quartz clocks and watches, **24**, 31, 33, 34, 82

relationships, time for, 62
Ronalds, Francis, 31
Rosbash, Michael, 41

Saltmarshe, Ella, 76
sandglass, 28
Seedling Project, **68**, 78
Seiko watches, 33, 35
shadow clocks
about, 17–19, 26, 27, 82
and sundials, 26, 82
and term 'clockwise', 27

siestas, **56**, 65, 82
Sinclair, David, 45
sleep research, 39–41, 43, 65
slow movement, the, 44, **56**, 63
smartwatches, **33**, 41
social networking, **41**, 61
solar cycle
  calendar, 16
  hours and minutes, 17–21
solar watches, 34
sports
  performance, 43, 63
  records, **57**, 58
standardized time
  atomic clocks, **14**, 21, 22, 34, 81
  daylight saving time, 2, 35, 81
  Greenwich Mean Time (GMT), **14**, 20, 81
  lunar time zone, **14**, 23
stress, 33, 60–61, 65, 67
striatum, 42, 82
subjective time. *See* perception of time
Sumerians, ancient, 17
sundials, 26, 82
sunlight and shadows, **14**, 17–19, 26
symbolism
  Father Time, **4**, 9
  the hourglass, 9, 28

tamarind trees, **46**, 48
technology
  and aging, **37**, 45
  GPS, 22, 34, 81
  jet-lag apps, **36**, 43
  lunar time zone, **14**, 23
  sleep apps, 65
  smartwatches, **33**, 41
  social networking, **41**, 61
  Y2K (year 2000) software problem, 75
tesseracts, 11
time
  cyclical, 62
  defined, 22
  learning to tell, 32
  linear, 6, 10, 13
  understanding of, 5–10
time blindness, 33, 82
time capsules, 35
time cells
  animals, **46**, 50–51
  human, 42–43
timefulness, 76, 82
time machines, 11, 12
time management
  and analog devices, 33
  and long-term planning, 69, 76–79
  work-life balance, 60
time sickness, **56**, 61, 82
time travel, 11–13
travel
  jet-lag, **36**, 43
  timekeeping, 28
  time zones, 20, **21**
tree planting, 78, **79**
trees
  internal clocks, 48
  rings, **46**, 53
Triumph of Truth, The (Rubens), 9

Urd, Norse goddess, 8

WALL-E (movie), 74
watches
  electric, **31**
  first pocket, **25**
  mechanical, 29, 30, 82
  quartz, **24**, 33
water clocks, **24**, 27, 35, 82
Whyte, Kyle Powys, 62
Wrinkle in Time, A (L'Engle), **4**, 11

Y2K (year 2000) software problem, 75
Young, Michael W., 41

Zombies (movie), 74
zombie movies, 74, 82
Zoroastrianism, 7, 82

From the PAST to the PRESENT and into the FUTURE!

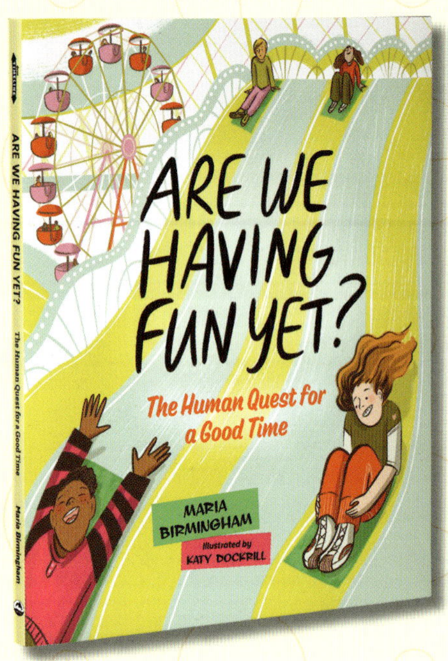

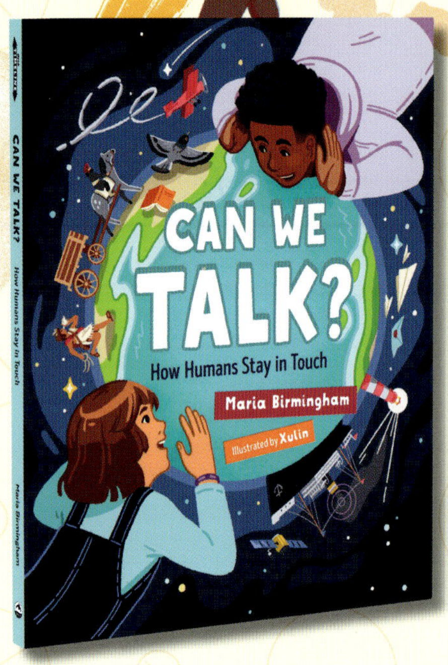

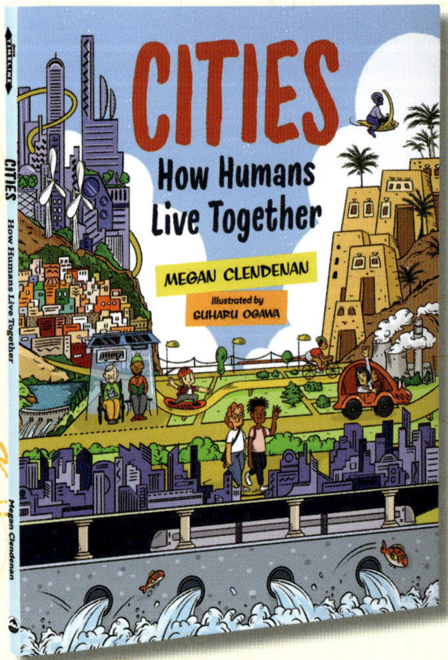

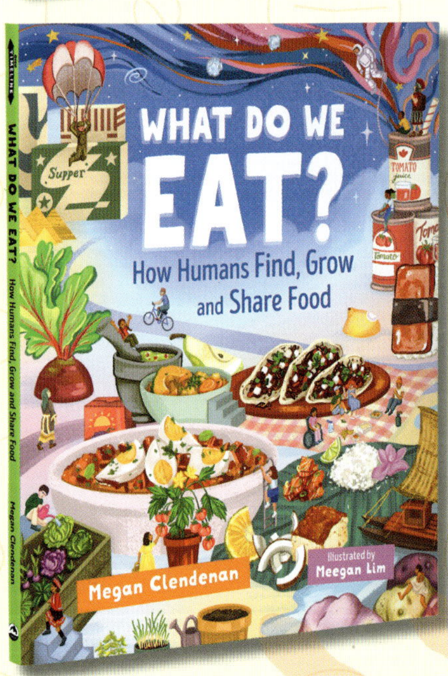

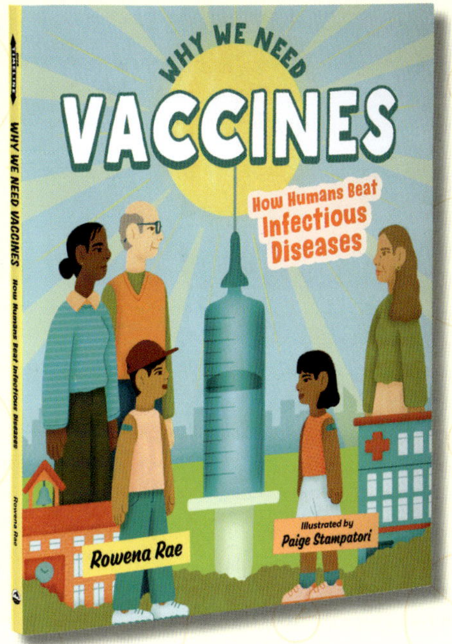

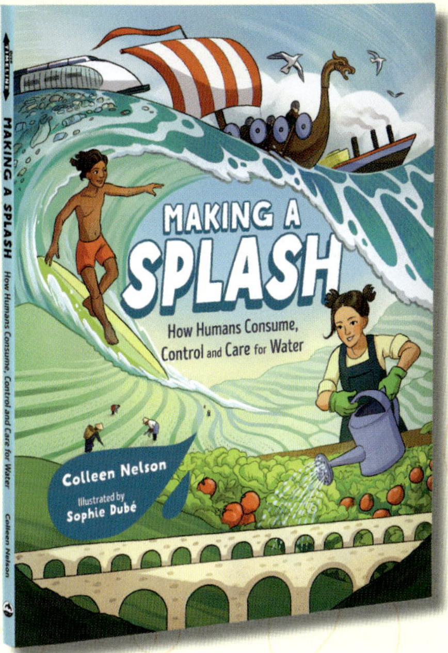

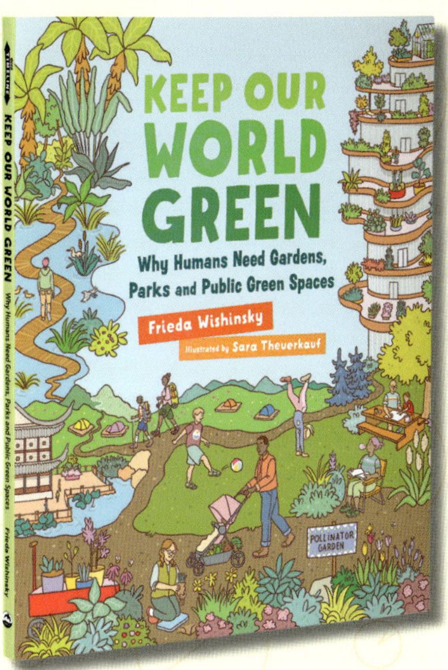

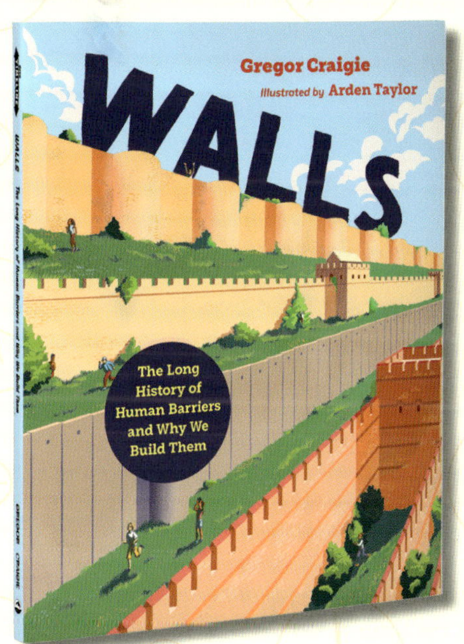

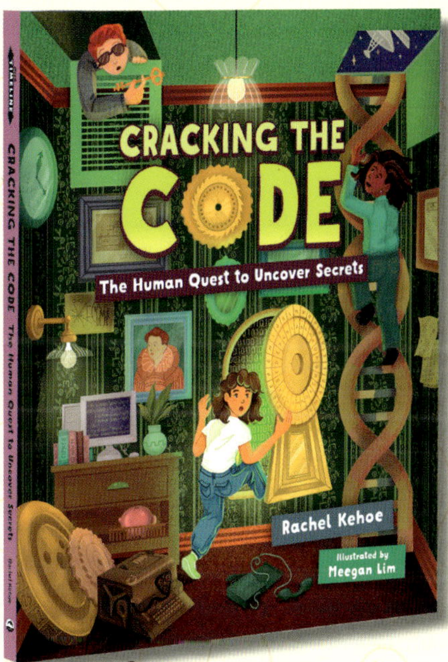

The Orca Timeline series explores how big ideas have shaped humanity. Discover what our collective history can tell us about the planet today and tomorrow.

KEN WILKINSON

Kirstie Hudson is an award-winning writer, editor and journalist. She was a long-time reporter and producer with CBC Radio. Kirstie coauthored two books with Indigenous artist Carey Newman. *Picking Up the Pieces* was a finalist for the City of Victoria Butler Book Prize. *The Witness Blanket* was the winner of the Norma Fleck Award for Canadian Children's Non-Fiction and a finalist for the TD Canadian Children's Literature Award. As an instructor at the University of Victoria, Kirstie shared her love of storytelling with students in writing and journalism. She lives in Victoria, BC.

JOHN FREDRICKS

Monique Polak is the author of over 30 books for young people. She is a three-time winner of the Quebec Writers' Federation Prize for Children's and YA Literature, now called the Janet Savage Blachford Prize. Monique taught for 35 years at Marianopolis College in Montreal. She is also a freelance journalist whose stories have appeared frequently in the *Montreal Gazette* and in Postmedia publications across Canada. Her previous nonfiction titles include *I Am a Feminist*, *Why Humans Work* and *Open Science: Knowledge for Everyone*. Monique does writing workshops for kids and adults across the country. She lives in Montreal.

Paige Stampatori is an illustrator based in Kitchener, Ontario. She graduated from Sheridan College's honors illustration program in 2020. Paige is the illustrator of *Why We Need Vaccines: How Humans Beat Infectious Diseases*.